STEVE MULLINS

Yorkshire
The Case for Independence
A FEASIBILITY STUDY

The White Rose – Yorkshire's Emblem

The Harebell – Yorkshire's Flower

Published by New Generation Publishing in 2020

First Edition

ISBN
  Paperback 978-1-80031-899-1
  Ebook   978-1-80031-892-2

www.newgeneration-publishing.com

Table of Contents

Disclaimers

I have endeavoured to ensure information is current, accurate and appropriate; however, things change and priorities get reassigned.

I cannot warrant or represent the completeness, accuracy or fitness for purpose of the material provided here when used by a third party – you will have to conduct your own research, as you see appropriate, and reach your own conclusions.

This book is not a substitute for professional advice and the author will not be held liable for any damages, losses or consequential losses arising from using the material in this publication for any purpose whatsoever.

Over the course of fifty or so years I have attended lectures, joined groups, taken memberships and argued with lots of people – many of whom sparked some of the ideas and conclusions presented here. I have not kept meticulous notes and if I have failed to acknowledge anyone please get in touch and I will rectify the matter in the next edition.

The thought, approaches and calculations are mine alone and I take full responsibility for any inaccuracies or mis-representations and will take whatever corrective action is required in the next edition.

Acknowledgements

My son Tom for some very constructive comments and thoughts about the foundation, ethics and shape of the party.

Ann Stafford for encouragement, comments and corrections to grammar.

Michael Guy for the photo of the harebell.

And to all of you who have argued and disagreed with me or taken the time to read and constructively criticise the content of this proposal – even if your politics are at odds with the sentiments expressed here. You know who you are and I thank you all.

The Map of Britain 1972 is reproduced without permission; I was unable to remember the original publication and have failed to get in touch with the author. If the owners of the map wish to have it removed or to be acknowledged, please let me know and I'll amend the section in subsequent editions.

Preface

As a manager with some years of adding real value to organisations by transforming things (like milk to cheese), growing market share (taking products abroad), improving efficiencies and developing new products, I have been increasingly dismayed with the performance of banks and corporates (encouraged by the politicians) who focus on share prices to increase their notional value for the benefit of the few; but more of this later.

A real bugbear has been the encouragement (or lack of discouragement) by politicians of investment schemes, bundled sub-prime investments, lies, the growth of tax avoidance in selected countries, 'living' behind brass plaques and transfer pricing, to name a few of the processes adopted to deny society the investment it has worked to create.

For me, this came to a head in 2008 when the whole canker-ridden edifice masquerading as responsible investment houses collapsed. The banksters[1] running the schemes kept their ludicrous bonuses and the whole rotten creation was bailed out by those who got damaged in the process, overseen by the politicians (*of the people!*) who have yet to legislate, condemn or sanction those involved[2].

---

[1] A term first heard on The Kaiser Report on *Russia Today*.

[2] Other than removing the ex-CEO of RBS Fred Goodwin's knighthood in 2013. Some five years after he did so much damage to so many.

I produced a paper at the time, included as an appendix, to lay out my concerns; concerns which have been growing ever since.

Equally insidious is that with increasing wealth for the few comes increasing inequality for the many, as greater shares of (ever-rising) GDP are unequally distributed; and, with this comes other inequalities for the wealthy:

- Let off criminal charges,
- Higher interest rates on deposits,
- Easy access to law-makers to ensure favourable legislation,
- Tax avoidance schemes,
- Preferential lending.

And, governments do nothing to mitigate the situation, perhaps because the members of government (politicians – *of the people* remember) are themselves involved somehow (unspecified).

I tried to analyse my own mood and believe it was one, not of jealousy, but of indignation that these travesties were allowed to happen and were even being promoted to the detriment of society.

I also realised that while government focus is on increasing the wealth of the few (which promotes inequality) it is at the same time committed to fighting poverty. The net effect is to hollow out the middle and working classes – the very people who create tangible value.

In my own mind, until recently, I had confused the fight against poverty (which has worked) with the reduction in inequality (which hasn't).

These two forces, acting together, drive a growth in GDP that is not commensurate with one of the purposes of government – to improve the lot of the people you represent.

It is also salutary that as national power becomes concentrated in the hands of the few (Putin, Kim, Bolsonaro, Xi, Trump and others) the levels of inequality grow but the powerful justify this by the reducing poverty levels in the country.

Since 2008, things have got even sillier; perhaps culminating in the nonsense over Brexit where the Labour party saw fit to deny the referendum vote, and to block anything that might conceivably be constructive.

After several years of this nonsense and a couple of elections we had had enough and in 2019 held yet another election where I was sufficiently annoyed to stand as an Independent and lost my deposit (plus a few bob more) – but, learned a great deal in the process, so a worthwhile exercise.

Paul Romer, for a short time the chief economist at the World Bank, advocates bringing together in the same location like-minded people to argue and generate new ideas and opportunities, locations which he called *Charter Cities*.

What I have tried to do in this small proposal is to highlight some of the inadequacies of centralised party government and, rather than simply criticise, try to offer some constructive thoughts which are brought together as a working model for an independent Yorkshire.

I argue that Yorkshire is as much a state of mind as it is a county – a collection of like minds who can disagree creatively and amicably in order to bring a bit of common sense to the table.

An independent Yorkshire may be regarded as something like a Charter City – but a bit bigger. The argument is laid out below.

I hope you enjoy the proposal and, as always, I welcome constructive feedback.

Steve Mullins.

March 2020.

The Prologue

Governments all around the world are failing the people they purport to represent and care for. As far as I can establish this is because one of their foci is on ever-rising GDP as an economic necessity.

In the days when we had active Trades Unions, they ensured a fairer (but still unequal) distribution of the wealth generated by the work of the people. This worked because the company and the people occupied pretty much the same geographic space.

The more enlightened governments recognised the poverty that was around and set out to bring people above the bread-line.

Meantime, other than a few enlightened mill-owners, the industrial barons continued to abstract wealth from the efforts of the workforce; some of which found its way back into the local community through additional jobs in the Mill-Owner's mansion or designer garden. 'Trickle-down Economics' sort of worked because of physical proximity. Now it's a figment of an old professor's imagination or taught from an obsolete book.

Government didn't then and doesn't now address inequality; perhaps because there isn't a parliament in the world that isn't the home of the (sometimes very) wealthy, and why should they want to stop their own flow of riches? (at the expense of the poorer members of society – provided these poorer members don't actually fall into poverty or rise up).

Government statistics are based, generally, on ratios, changes and percentages; it can be quite difficult to get to the actual numbers, especially when there is change.

This difficulty in assessing the real figures (despite assurances of transparency) make it increasingly easy for the 'spin doctors' and PR companies to provide coverage that confuses inequality[3] with poverty and allows the self-interested to continue without much challenge.

We need to fight both poverty <u>and</u> inequality. One option considered later is to replace Corporation Tax with the (now defunct) Purchase Tax which, thanks to modern technology, can be monitored and taken at point of sale – thus being made available to provide benefits for the community which actually delivers profit to the supplier and not for the few individuals holed up somewhere in a tax-haven or a head office in a 'tax efficient' country.

Borrowing needs to be curtailed; and calculation shows that Yorkshire can take from local tax what we need to spend socially; there is no need to borrow against projected income – a process embedded in Whitehall and one that continues to drive increasing indebtedness.

The money supply needs to be better regulated, we used to have the gold standard until the reserves were sold for less than their net worth just before the price multiplied something like threefold. There are several good books about gold[4] and its use as a standard.

---

[3] A recent study by the US Bureau of Labor Statistics 2017 shows that the share of GDP paid to the labour force is actually falling [I believe this is stoking inequality.]

[4] See James Rickards who makes *The New Case for Gold.*

Some similar measure needs to be adopted to stop the banks simply printing more money, creating more debt and supporting the balance by government 'assets'[5].

Yet, there are still economists who argue that borrowing is a good thing – possibly because it keeps notional share values rising and with this an increase in notional value – the notional wealth of the few[6].

Focus needs to move from ever-rising GDP (the God of the economists for so many years) to real investment in society.

This supposed need for ever-increasing GDP is promoted by the support of the media with their inexorable *market reports*; the argument about pensions and the like should hold little water because each share delivers a dividend which pays the pension itself.

All this focus achieves is to justify the wealth gap and the inequality that this gap promotes.

Immigration will play a part because of our level of hospitality and agricultural activities. Banerjee and Duflo[7] demonstrate that immigration does not undermine the local economy but actually strengthens it and should (with a few caveats) be a normal part of society.

---

[5] See Ryan-Collins, Greenham, Werner & Jackson *Where does money come from?*

[6] About 15% of people own stocks and shares; the other 85% go along with increasing the notional wealth of the minority.

[7] bit.Banerjee & Duflo *Good Economics for Hard Times*.

The proposed UK immigration criteria are (at the time of writing) to have a £25k job to come to, plus other qualification, which is of little help to basic wage agriculture or hospitality – surely better to use a referral system of some sort.

Such a referral system might be where two people already here vouch for another to join them to work. If one apple proves to be bad the entire barrel goes back – the idea is that an immigrant offender, and sponsors, will be returned home (regardless of human rights claims – see later) with passport confiscated, irises scanned and fingerprints taken in order to prevent re-entry.

Given the scenario developed here, there is no need to strive for inexorably rising GDP in order to improve the lot of the community; merely that it stays more or less constant and is better distributed.

The following notes try to tackle several issues that are not necessarily compatible and whose emphasis changes from location to location and in time. It has been very difficult to develop a smooth narrative and occasionally the story jumps around a bit.

Please read this proposal as one of putting the pieces on the chess board and one possible version of the game described. Different game plays will emerge in time and may prove better than the one presented here, but please stick with it; I believe you will find the journey worthwhile.

Justification

We are currently beset with vanity projects (HS2), crumbling architecture (the Palace of Westminster), improvements that will benefit just the south east (third runway at Heathrow) and a few daft ideas (a bridge between Scotland and Ireland).

These 'initiatives' will effectively cost Yorkshire some £16bn[8] and with nothing to show for them, yet we have suffered from underfunding for decades – what with clapped out sprinter trains, the *Trans? Pennine "Express"*, the A64, some of the worst road surfaces in England and with communities isolated.

And, that's before we explore inequality: for example, in education the average spend per pupil in England is £5,328 per annum. In London this becomes £5,872 and in Yorkshire c.£5,070 – 5% below the average and 14% below London[9].

We are ignored; for example, *Fracking* was a major issue yet the wishes of the parliamentary party and about 30 votes far overwhelmed the local community with several hundred votes against.

Interestingly, some 30 years or so ago, oil was found beneath Windsor Great Park; much more readily extractable and more useful than shale gas but, strangely, no-one seems now to mention this rich source of energy which could be quite readily extracted.

---

[8] Roughly £6,500 per household; or over two years' supply of beer for every person in the county.

[9] Derived from quite obscure government figures: Schools_Pupils_and_their_Characteristics_2019:

The Accompanying Tables.

The inequalities continue to build and whilst being expected to pay £16bn. we are supposed to say 'thank-you' for a minor share of a £5bn national handout (over five years – £1bn p.a. nationally, or c.£125m. to Yorkshire) to tart up the buses.

More recently, traffic police have halved in Yorkshire but doubled in the Met Police area[10]; surely the population there hasn't doubled and, what about the improvements to road and rail in the south east? I guess the MPs find it easier to get to work though.

– We are still picking up the crumbs from beneath the rich man's table.

Without putting too fine a point on it, Westminster has cared little about managing the good of the people; as easily demonstrated by:

- The NI savings were plundered some years ago – in commerce this is an indictable offence.
- WASPI women[11], no need to elaborate here.
- Universal Credit; £15bn (and rising) spent on an IT infrastructure that is still not right.
- An increase in public sector staff from about 3.5m workers to 5.25m workers – an immediate additional cost of £42bn which persists to this day and will grow because of pension demands; yet justified by these extra

---

[10] *Inside Out* a local TV news programme.
[11] Women Against State Pension Inequality.

workers paying tax which is OK for this year but who pays them next year?

Duck houses, chandeliers and subscriptions to porn sites pale into insignificance against this vandalism. And, so it continues with HS2, bridges, third runways and the rest.

Yet no-one gets properly fired – just moved to the comfort of the back benches and £80,000+ a year.

An inescapable fact

Never has Yorkshire independence been more important as power and wealth across the globe becomes increasingly concentrated in the hands of the few:

A few politicians: Jair Bolsonaro, Kim Jong Un, Xi Jinping, Vladimir Putin, Donald Trump and now Boris Johnson.

A few organisations: Banks, Pharma, Weapons, Oil, IT, Computers and Space.

A few business people: Jeff Bezos, Bill Gates, Warren Buffett and Mark Zuckerberg.

The balance has tipped too far from the people who support (and pay) these people and the money these organisations and individuals manage to keep for themselves.

The balance needs to tip back in the direction of those who have been disadvantaged by the growing inequality; and the way to tip that balance is for the people (of Yorkshire) to become self-sufficient. That is what I have tried to tackle here.

Conclusion

The arguments continue to build for an independent county that stops propping up the elite, the greedy and the profligate and actually begins to look after the interests of its own people.

[My paraphrase] *Never in the history of social economics have so few spent so much to deliver so little to so many.*

I make no apologies for repeating this later.

It is now time for us to stand up for what ought to be ours through a political party specific to Yorkshire – one which we will have to work hard on in preparation for the next election.

However, when it comes to voting, peoples' minds are made up as to which <u>package</u> they prefer[12] and the time is now right to create an integrated package for Yorkshire and make it widely known throughout the county.

I believe this feasibility study demonstrates that an Independent Yorkshire is perfectly possible.

---

[12] Occasionally, which package they do not prefer, e.g. the Labour party at the 2019 elections when a number of safe Labour seats were 'won' by the Conservatives.

The argument

It is better to aim high and miss than aim low and hit – Les Brown.

There are: The Yorkshire Party, The Independents of North Yorkshire Party and The For Britain Movement, for Yorkshire Party. However, none of them seem to have made much of a mark and are focused on gaining traction in Westminster when a few voices amongst 650 are unlikely to be heard.

The litany of under-investment by Whitehall has examples from every walk of life: health, schools, industry, energy, infrastructure – the list goes on.

Yorkshire is robust enough to stand on its own and should sue for independence. This will not come easily or immediately but is worth fighting for.

In this thesis I argue that Yorkshire can be self-sufficient financially with its own well-defined boundaries (rivers and the Pennines) and should be able to direct its own money to where it is most appropriate on a local level.

There is also a case to be made for changes to governance and the management structure, and also to taxation. These are laid out in some detail later.

The inability of political parties to quantify investment policies was made clear in the main party manifestos – just about each one was considered pie in the sky by the Institute of Fiscal Studies (IFS); yet the likes of current politicians, who have very ably demonstrated an inability to add up or do basic arithmetic, roundly denounced the IFS and 'getting their sums wrong'. I beg to differ and offer a basic business case below.

People don't vote for change; they vote against uncertainty.

The way to generate certainty is through self-sufficiency. We should aim high with clear purpose and a defined target. In this discussion I lay out that clear purpose – a better future for the citizens of the County of Yorkshire, bought and paid for by their own endeavour.

It is possible to achieve this aim under current conditions with a few changes (e.g. structure of governance, taxation) and to have in place a *Mission* and an *Objective* with which to drive our *Strategy* – to maintain course even when external events outside our control force change, for example fuel prices. This *Strategy* will replace the usual *Manifesto* which is rarely much more than an ill-thought-out wish list to try to win a few more votes.

Time for another party

The situation with the established Yorkshire parties is that they do not seem prepared to aim high enough and their manifestos and promises focus on gaining some sort of presence in Parliament which, even with 40 or so seats, would be minimal at best. The Yorkshire Party fielded 8 candidates in 2019 – potentially about 1½% of all MPs. (the expression *farting against the thunder* comes easily to mind).

This minimal presence is nowhere near enough to influence a treasury focused on the South-east and the Yorkshire Party manifesto promises of major expenditure on remediation are just that – little more than promises.

For example, the Yorkshire Party promises to spend:

£39bn on rail (the original cost of HS2!),

23,000 new homes each year, conservatively £50,000 per dwelling – per annum: £1.25bn,

£5.250 per pupil, an increase of £180, hardly significant and not even up to national average; yet it found its way into the manifesto as if it was something significant.

There are no estimates of any expenditure in a number of key areas that include: infrastructure beyond rail, health, policing, industry, agriculture, areas of outstanding natural beauty, energy generation and energy usage (in all its various forms) or higher education & training; there are allusions to devolution of services such as health but no attempt to create a business case.

One of the problems with the smaller parties and independents is that there is no certainty that the promises made can, or will, be delivered.

Without control over income, there can be no control over expenditure and a caucus of 8 amongst 650 hardly represents an opportunity to take control. The manifesto was just not believable.

However, at the 2019 elections the Yorkshire Party beat three independents (me included) despite no literature and no presence at the hustings. The lesson is clear, *people vote for parties, not for people.*

Yorkshire is resilient enough to manage as an Independent State and the inescapable conclusion is that The Yorkshire Party, to be successful, would need to significantly raise its sights and to get its act together – neither of which seem likely – so a new and independent party needs to be founded.

I argue for a second representative party to be founded with people who have the vision, the experience and a mind-set that is focused on co-operation not personal progress at any cost (this is discussed below).

This is appropriate because established local politicians' natural instinct is to resist change in any form and fight to maintain the status quo[13]; they also avoid anything that might smack of a risk – however minor – because this might blow their veneer of infallibility. No risk, no change. Try admitting you got it wrong, learn and move forward. It works.

There are also numerous examples of politicians, once elected, toeing the party line even if that means ignoring the needs, lifestyles and livelihoods of the communities that elected them.

The original aim was to found The Yorkshire Independent Party – but YIP lends itself to confusion with the Wae'aye Party which risks a northerly bias at the expense of the rest of the county, even though the title is perhaps more accurate. So instead I propose The Yorkshire Democratic Party – where, thankfully, there are few

---

[13] Described elsewhere as *aggressive mediocrity.*

confusing acronyms for YDP even though the use of the word *Democratic* smacks of a totalitarian state.

Plan Overview

A very broad outline of a plan is set out below; the detail will be more fully developed later with a greater range of interests, inputs and experiences[14].

One of the key aspects of this plan is that it addresses both poverty and inequality; governments of all persuasions, both here and abroad, have addressed poverty whilst allowing inequality to continue to rise. This increase in inequality is shown by increasing GDP but with stagnating wages – the banks are printing money to shore up ever-worsening stock markets.

Where rising GDP was once a means to an end, it has now become an end in itself which results in increasing government borrowing and increasing debt – a Ponzi scheme by any other name, discussed further below.

The vision, mission, objective and strategy are set out more fully below under 'Creating Yorkshire's Road-map'.

Phase 1

Between now and the 2024/5 election.

---

[14] Experience is something that comes just slightly too late to be of practical use.

The scenario is that things will get worse before they get better which will result in increasing disenchantment with party politicians. During this period the YDP needs to become widely known.

The main drive will be to establish a cadre of candidates, preferably with political experience and for the key interested people to finalise the finances and structure of the party across the county.

Create a website with a simple, easy to follow manifesto and a more complete document for those who are sufficiently interested. This may be further developed into a social network which can be readily accessed and views shared (it will need overseeing though and that might come later).

Set up as many funding streams as possible (it is quite an expensive business to stand against the establishment. I know) and engage wealthy sponsors and Yorkshire firms keen to support the county and their brand with the harebell[15] which would have to be officially registered as the party emblem.

The party will need an agent who knows the ins and outs of the various bits of legislation that go around an election to ensure we can play the game to maximum effect.

With the finances agreed and a manifesto finalised to actively, <u>and positively</u>, challenge the local party MPs (it's no good rubbishing what they are standing for; there needs to be a positive attack – *But why have you not taken xxx into consideration? It would significantly improve the local services by ...) / wouldn't it have been more*

---

[15] The harebell is officially the flower of Yorkshire.

sensible to ... drawing into the argument the points in the YDP manifesto and strategy.

To identify people who are both telegenic and photogenic to appear wherever possible on local TV – the rest of us can appear on radio.

Ensure these challenges are reported in the local press and in local social media; ideally, asking for local newsworthy contributions.

With luck, there will be celebrities wanting to become involved which will boost both their and our TV exposure and desirability.

The aim is to build a significant positive party presence so that for the year before the next election YDP can compete on an equal footing with the established parties.

Having established that it can be done there will be, hopefully, half a dozen or so people who will be elected to Westminster.

Phase 2

Between the 2024/5 and the 2029/30 elections.

Now that we have shown that it is possible to gain seats in Parliament and that we have a winning team the attack now becomes two-pronged: One section working to grow discontent with the local traditional party politicians and the other prong creating a fuss in Westminster (YDP can learn from the SDP).

A Central Oversight office that co-ordinates things and ensures equality between Constituencies made up of past Independent Candidates who have felt strongly enough to spend their own money to try to put things to rights. I suggest 9 such individuals – three from each Riding (the original divisions of Yorkshire[16]) for a term of three years, one retiring each year to be replaced or re-elected by the elected Members.

64 Constituencies united into 16 groups of four, each of the 16 groups representing an area, or areas; for example, all four Members might represent a city, or a disparate four might represent rural interests.

Each constituency to stand for four years with a Representative elected by the Members plus a Deputy, the Representative retires after a year and the Deputy takes over as the next Representative with their Deputy who will become the next Representative.

The Deputies to be appointed in their second year of office, the Representatives to be appointed in their third year.

The *County Quorum* will consist of nine elected past Independent Candidates (three from each Riding) and sixteen group representatives.

Additional to this, the individual Constituents will be linked to their elected Member electronically (with a bespoke app) and will be encouraged to participate in voting where there are priorities to be determined.

---

[16] Originally: North, East & West, derived from Old English: Thriding – a third.

This is very much at odds with the current system where the party in power votes for all electors who have bought into a package of measures – whether right for their particular circumstances or not[17].

It has been remarked that *Direct Democracy* frightens the parties because the leader is not in charge any more (cf. the original Brexit referendum). The switch here is from an MP with privilege and little responsibility to a Member with responsibility and actually earning the privileges.

- Constituent
- Member
- Group
- Deputy
- Representative
- Quorum

By providing connectivity and an appropriate app people can be as engaged as they wish to be and in a position to support, suggest amendments or criticise the local decisions being made.

The intent is to become semi-detached and to be in a position to offer suggestions about governance; for example taxation, and to give Westminster the opportunity to use Yorkshire as a proving ground, so that later our own scheme of taxation will have been developed, problems identified and the various taxes can be introduced smoothly in phase three.

---

[17] The expression *Package Manifesto* is from Martin Cruttwell who stood as an Independent in 2016.

The level of discontent with London-based politics and a positive approach, coupled with several MPs in post in Westminster will lend credibility to the party for the next election.

As with phase one, there will be a drive to broadcast the YDP message widely and loudly, increasing the volume about a year out from the election.

The target will be to get more than half of the Yorkshire candidates established in the House of Commons.

Phase 3

Between the 2029/30 and the 2034/5 elections.

HS2 should be running to Birmingham by now and can be used as a means to demonstrate how little benefit it has brought the north – and at what cost to necessary local projects.

The poor management of northern finances plus a projected growing discontent with the party system (fuelled over the last ten years) should open the door to independence.

Governance would be similar to Westminster but with appropriately experienced people who have the experience and strength of character to make decisions and admit when they get them wrong.

An Unelected Chamber

Made up of: CEO, MD, Chair; and appropriate others selected from, for example: the workforce, industrialists who pay full Yorkshire taxes, people from education and supporters of the rural economy.

The target is to get a genuine cross-section of the society at large with skills and experience balanced against the growing needs of the county.

Their main role is to get the planning right[18] to ensure funds and expertise will be available to the Constituencies and applied as appropriate now and into the future.

The principle will be that of William Shipley when he established the Royal Society of Arts (Manufactures & Commerce) over 250 years ago – an impartial forum where people from different backgrounds, disciplines and interests could freely gather, meet, discuss, share and learn for mutual benefit and for the benefit of society as a whole.

The Elected Chamber

Made up of people chosen by their various Constituencies – the politicians (of the people remember) who represent the diverse interests of their various communities.

---

[18] Including scenario planning.

What is Yorkshire?

Yorkshire is more than a county, it's a state of mind, like other stand-out UK tribes that include: Geordies, Cockneys, the Cornish, the Welsh and the Scots.

Tha' can tek the person out of Yorkshire but tha'll nivver tek the Yorkshire out o' the person.

That said, Yorkshire, for the uninitiated, is a county of some 4,500 square miles with a population of 5.4 million and 2.47 persons per household – about the same as Scotland.

If Yorkshire were a state on its own within the EU it would come about 18th out of 26 by population.

As a country in its own right we would have finished 27th in the medals table at the Rio Olympics, ahead of South Africa, New Zealand and Canada.

There are traits and characters that are equal to, or better than, those exhibited elsewhere in the UK (or even the world!). These include: character, inspirational people, sport, creativity, music, entertainment, science & invention.

Here, to set the scene is a brief summary:

Character

Rather than take many pages to dissect what Yorkshire is, here are a few brief thoughts which summarise some of the main points; there are many supportive pages to be accessed on the web.

Pride – in the county, in countrymen, in work professionally completed and delivered on time.

To the Point – often misunderstood by Southern people as rudeness; it's an approach that says it like it is, avoids misunderstanding and is a rejection of hyperbole, deviousness and obfuscation.

Thrift – often regarded as meanness with long pockets and short arms, however the Yorkshire person can be, and is, most liberal with money when the reason for laying it out seems clearly to be a strong and a valid one. Few people are as generous (in private!) with friends and colleagues.

Importantly, this thrift goes beyond money to include administration, meetings, negotiation and management. People know what is required of them and when.

Tenacity – once an idea is embedded it takes an awfully good argument or alternative to shake it loose: *tha' can allus tell a Yorkshireman, but tha' can't tell him much.* Sometimes referred to as stubbornness, other times as tenacity.

Cheerful negativity – even the worst of situations have an ironic or even a funny side, this can be misconstrued by southerners but, given a tough upbringing, it's one way to build resilience.

Tender hearted underneath – whilst people will keep themselves to themselves, if someone needs a hand it is freely given – and without any expectation of a return favour (the 'favour bank' seems to be a southern invention).

Inspirational People

Yorkshire has produced outstanding people in every sphere of endeavour, including percussive expertise (Guy Fawkes), and can act as inspiration to the new independent members; the short summary below demonstrates the strength in depth that can be called upon to deliver outstanding value to the county.

Sport

There are many examples. The more complete lists are much longer, but here are some names to conjure with or bring back memories.

Cricket – David Bairstow, Geoffrey Boycott, Len Hutton, Katie Brunt, Joe Root, Laura Spragg.

Football – Brian Clough, Kevin Keegan, Rachel Daly, Beth Mead, Steve McClaren, David Seaman.

Athletics – The Brownlee brothers, Jessica Ennis, Nicola Adams, Hannah Cockroft, Brian Noble, Ed Clancey.

Creativity

Yorkshire people have contributed to each and every facet of culture and creativity (despite being painted as uncouth, uncommunicative and lacking feeling!)

Sculpture – Henry Moore, Robert Thompson, Barbara Hepworth.

Fine Art – David Hockney, Damien Hirst, Robert Fuller, Lucy Pittaway.

Literature – the Brontës, Ian McMillan, Margaret Drabble, Alan Bennett, Barbara Taylor Bradford, Henry Fielding, Ted Hughes, J. B. Priestley.

Music and Entertainment

Brass bands – Black Dyke, Brighouse and Rastrick, Grimethorpe Colliery and many others.

Pop – Arctic Monkeys, Susan Maughan, Joe Cocker, Def Leppard, Pulp, Robert Palmer, Tasmin Archer, Arthur Brown, The Beautiful South to name a few.

Classical – Dame Janet Baker, Lesley Garrett.

Composers – Frederick Delius, Haydn Wood, John Barry, Katie Chatburn, George Dyson.

Entertainment – Jeremy Clarkson, Roy Castle, Molly Sugden, Adrian Edmondson, Bob Mortimer, Frankie Howerd and Charlie Williams – one of the first black football players and stand-up comedians.

Actors – Brian Blessed, Dame Diana Rigg, Sir Ben Kingsley, Charles Laughton, Dame Judi Dench.

Science and Invention

A good many inventions, discoveries, science and scientific theories have originated from Yorkshire; here are just a few:

- Harry Brearley – invented stainless steel.

- Henry Briggs – developed logarithms.
- Sir George Cayley – manned flight etc.
- Amy Johnson – aviator.
- Helen Sharman – the first British astronaut.
- Joseph Priestley – discovered oxygen.
- Sir Fred Hoyle – rejected the big bang.

The list goes on with mouse traps, cats' eyes, loft ladders (the millionth UK patent) and the rest.

It should not be forgotten that just about all the outputs from those mentioned above (and those not mentioned) are, or have been, capable of further development, export and sale.

This creativity can be developed into centres of technological excellence; there are nearly 50 further and higher education centres in the county and as earnings depend increasingly on technology, the skills and aptitudes of those people who invented the touch screen (Hull), motion pictures and Jelly Tots can be better harnessed and nurtured.

A conglomerate called Top Tech Yorkshire is already judging and celebrating new technology in the county.

Some of Yorkshire's Assets

There are a significant number of assets that can be used to build a sustainable and self-governing community, a number have already been mentioned but to put them into readily identifiable groups there are:

- Coastal ports – export, foreign trade and
        potentially tax-free zones,
- Innovative and inventive people,
- A thirst for industry,

- 12 universities,
- 37 colleges,
- We know what work is,
- Established business parks,
- Extensive agriculture,
- Major manufacturers,
- Sports, stables and racing,
- Wind, water and waves (for clean energy),
- Natural resources e.g. potash,
- Areas of Outstanding Natural Beauty,
- Tourism,
- Industrial parks already established.

All are capable of further 'clean' development and exploitation for the good of the county.

Borders and boundaries

We have the benefit of a couple of big rivers north and south, a mountain range to the west that is about 110 miles long and the sea to the east, an easily recognised and distinct area (other than a couple of anomalies that will no doubt prove to be remarkably troublesome as we gain independence).

For reference Hadrian's wall is 84 miles long which is a bit less than we would need; but let's learn from the Scots who got it right so long ago.

The technology exists to police these boundaries with number-plate recognition (already in use), facial recognition (or something similar, which will no doubt have the bugs ironed out in time) and personal GPS embedded in just about every smart phone. This emerging technology needs to be harnessed and focused.

Financial Overview

The finances are more fully developed later but some of the changes and key points that lead to a balanced economy and obtaining the funds to meet the goals of the manifesto are noted below.

One of the benefits and also one of the bugbears of today's economy is *connectedness* whereby companies can set up shop wherever is most tax efficient. Companies can route sales and purchases through an overseas head office to avoid UK tax and maximise the dividend to an already wealthy individual; all to the detriment of the society in which the organisation trades and which supported it. This manipulation of corporation tax and income tax is the avoidance of an obligation to society. The relationships between government, industry and society are developed more fully later as an appendix.

On the positive side, connectedness also makes it possible to compare prices around the globe (e.g. the holiday bookers) which can be adapted to sales of all products and services without fear or favour – even the manufacturers of baby items, pharmaceuticals and items that are zero-rated for VAT need to make a profit to stay in business and remain competitive.

To overcome this avoidance of corporation tax, due to 'offshoring' and other financial wheezes, corporation tax will be replaced by purchase tax. The calculated level of purchase tax is based on work done some years ago by The Institute for

Business Ethics who calculated that the net profit (after interest, depreciation and 'fudge factors' etc.) for an ethically managed company as 8.2% of turnover[19]. Corporation tax is currently c.20% of profit.

The level of purchase tax is set to effectively collect the corporation tax that is due and set at 2.0% of all sales with checks and balances to identify prices that have been artificially inflated.

The total potential calculated income from all sources including Purchase Tax is £46.4bn; this is developed more fully later.

The calculated expenditure for the county, to properly improve infrastructure, maintain and improve the current overall level of services, based to some extent on total UK figures and on some conservative estimates, comes in at £46.5bn.

There is a small discrepancy (0.2%) but the income and expenditure are pretty much equal (which is what you might expect by more or less copying a UK treasury full of clever people doing the balancing act).

There are savings to be made with governance; current governmental budgeting – at all levels – has the notion that next year's budget will be the same as this year's spend plus a bit. We all have stories of government profligacy around January/February

---

[19] Institute for Business Ethics: Does Business Ethics Pay?

as departments spend up to budget in order to get next year's funds. Surely, this can be changed.

For example, with IT, there is a great deal of interest in Estonia[20] which has connected the entire country for about £100m. Compare this to the cost of IT for UK welfare payments which is currently running at £15bn – and growing. The golden rule is to keep politicians and their bright ideas out of the way[21]. This can be emulated.

Central government spends 43% of GDP on running costs, staff and admin; roughly twice what is needed to manage efficiently. This can be reduced.

The assumption is made that 20% of total income (c.£40bn for the county) should be spent on governance and administration, this is equal to £8bn and is consistent with the NYCC budget who do not have to support activities like the House of Lords for example. This can be maintained.

The simple expedient of zero-based budgeting will be introduced with allocations set against clearly defined objectives – objectives determined by area.

For example, it is perhaps more important for a town to have increased policing whilst a rural community might need a better bus service.

Specific areas will be able to decide their own priorities, unlike today where spending is capped or ring-fenced depending on party position. There will

---

[20] Professional manager; Spring 2019 pp.43-47.

[21] See *The Mythical Man Month* by Frederick Brookes, it's a bit old but still very true.

also be the opportunity to re-allocate budget underspend to where it will do the most good, for example to social housing.

Vanity projects such as HS2 will be sidelined until the county is generating sufficient surplus to consider such initiatives; infrastructure will continue to be addressed with connectivity between towns and cities a priority which has been budgeted for.

Ponzi budgeting – a digression

Many years ago, in America (where else) Charles Ponzi landed in Boston as a petty criminal and chancer. He established a scheme where he promised fantastic interest rates on money invested in his company (The Securities Exchange Company) and paid sales agents large commissions for each new client.

The reason he was able to be so big-hearted was that sales income kept growing and interest payments were met from new incoming investments. Generous payments to sales people ensured there was a continual stream of willing depositors.

However, like all bubbles, it burst, with new depositors drying up and people started to ask for their capital back. The depositors' interest had been paid out with the money from new investors and without a continual flow of new investors the depositors lost their savings, some their houses and pensions – with a scheme that had seemed so good.

The current scheme of governmental financial management is no more than a Ponzi scheme, using borrowings one year to pay for last year's expenditure. We are digging an ever-deepening hole of debt[22].

Yet, despite the bubble-blowing antics of Charles Ponzi, there are economists who argue that borrowing is actually a good thing.

HS2 – 'Ow Much?'

I have singled out HS2 because, in the field of any sort of endeavour, rarely has such weak justification been used by so few to spend so much to do so little for so many.

Here is how the argument works (as explained by a northern MP toeing the party line over HS2 in a TV interview in January 2020).

[My paraphrase]. HS2 will link to northern rail systems and bring significant benefits to the north. The overall cost will be about £100bn and will link the entire country in about 17 years, which is a long time, so we ought to get stuck in now.

*With today's rates, the interest is only(!) about £2bn p.a. which is less than the calculated annual benefit. The project represents a very realistic cost / benefit outcome. **It's a no-brainer** [my emphasis].*

Yes, it does, until you take into account the need to repay the capital – £100bn and rising – and that

---

[22] Denis Healey, once Chancellor of the exchequer, had as the basic law of politics and finance: "when you're in a hole, stop digging". Apparently forgotten by the current financial teams.

the benefits do not arise until the bits from Birmingham to the north are completed in 2036 (and now slipping to 2040), if at all.

Assume the capital is repaid from 2036 onwards, which is when the calculated profitability kicks in (and let's also assume that global interest rates have stayed very modest – unlikely); the aggregated interest plus capital will be in excess of £150bn. If all the accumulated benefit is used to pay this back (assume £5bn p.a. net benefit, reduced to £2bn through continuing interest payments) it will take a further 65 years just to reach break-even – 2100.

However, party accounting being what it is, will no doubt project ever-increasing returns and borrow yet more money against these projections to fund the growing interest payments and perhaps promise to pay back some of the capital. These borrowings will then accrue further interest and so the spiral continues but, the people who concocted this scheme will be warmly retired and feather-bedded by then.

It appears that it is the party economist who is the 'no-brainer'; that, or a disciple of Charles Ponzi!

At the time of writing (early 2020) the Westminster government seem determined to push ahead with HS2 'to open up the North' – this is hogwash. The likelihood is that it will only go as far as Birmingham and then be 'reviewed' (is this as far north as some of our MPs have ever dared to venture? please see the map below), <u>perhaps</u> Manchester 15 years later and as the price continues to rise, will it still be important to connect Leeds and York when Northern Rail will, at last, be working efficiently? I doubt it.

And to add insult to injury, at the time of writing the government is talking to the Chinese about managing the construction – I wonder how much of your money will be used to fund the various penalty clauses of UK firms; money that will no doubt be wisely invested in the Caymen Islands.

Other future planned expenditure

There is the need to refurbish the Palace of Westminster (Parliament), estimated at £4bn plus an additional £2bn for temporary accommodation and there will surely arise opportunities to upgrade the IT systems and other services. This price will no doubt double.

There have been a number of arguments to support increased air traffic into the south-east (where the wealth is already concentrated) which will demand a third runway at Heathrow. This is likely to be decided in 2021 and no doubt will go ahead because of the likely benefit to the south east of England. The costs are a bit convoluted so here is an estimate (subject to the inevitable revision):

The scheme itself	£14.0bn
Access changes to the airport	£2.5bn
Monetising the carbon impact (!)	£1.0bn
In total	£17.5bn

There's a fair chance that this cost will also double if other capital schemes are in any way a barometer.

There is no indication whether this includes: the cost of repatriating the people of Harmondsworth, soundproofing houses under the new flightpath in Southall or funding the various penalty payments which will surely arise.

None of the benefit of this investment will come north, but talent and expertise that should be used for repairing the north will no doubt flow south, degrading the county even further.

And, even if linked to HS2 no-one will want to add at least two hours to their journey time getting to Euston to go on to the north (hopefully on business).

And now, talk of a bridge between Scotland and Ireland. For reference, the second Forth Bridge (The Queensferry Bridge) cost £5.4bn and is 1.7 miles long. The Scotland/Ireland bridge will be at least 12 miles long, not counting the upgrades to roads either side of the crossing and the technology needed to fight the tides, wind and dumped armaments. As an estimate – at least another £40bn – with no benefit to the north of England.

All of these initiatives will need funding, probably to the tune of a figure in excess of £200bn when it's all added up and the 'fudge factors' taken into account.

This funding must come from taxation and the proportion to be provided by Yorkshire will be of the order of £16bn – admittedly spread over a number of years. However, there will be no benefit whatsoever to the county and it's a fair bet that the South-east will not see any diminution of investment in their own back-yard.

Yet, in Yorkshire we still have sprinter trains 20 years out of date, the *Trans? Pennine "Express"* debacles, and Leeds is still the only major UK city without some form of Metro. The chances of upgrades still seem as remote as ever, even remoter if these proposed engineering initiatives come about and Westminster continues to drain funds in order to look after its own self-interested schemes.

Now is the time to manage our own finances and to stop pouring our hard-earned money into palaces and vanity projects.

The case for an independent Yorkshire is self-evident, clear and is set out below.

Basis for the Case

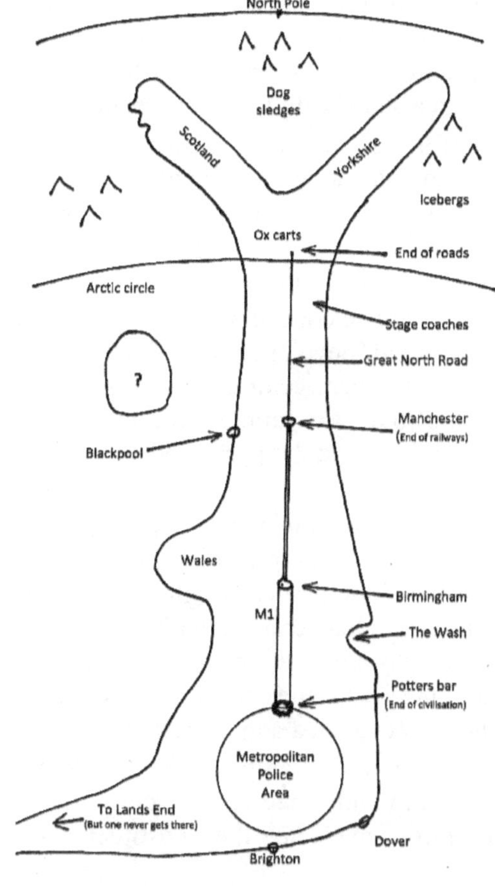

Ye newe map of Britain circa 1972

Recreated 2017

How Londoners see the North. This map of Great Britain is being sent out by Doncaster and District Development Council in a good humoured attempt to attract more industry to the North. It wasn't thought up though by Doncastrians, who actually believe Doncaster is the centre of Great Britain, and possibly the universe. It was thought up by Beatrice Urquhart a teacher at Doncaster's Notre Dame Grammar School, and she hails from Wimbledon. "I know a girl in London who came home one day, in tears and said "The department's moving up North, I've go to go to Harrogate. I don't know what will become of me."

Published in the national press and
As true today as fifty years ago.

In order to be effective, there needs to be co-ordination in government to ensure resources are realistically allocated and that the various elected representatives can fulfil their core responsibilities (see *The Purpose of Government?* Below). Without a degree of control and co-ordination there would be anarchy and a significant waste of resources.

This control has for very many years been mainly through managing the financial affairs of the realm which has resulted, generally, in the banks' head offices and decision-making centres being situated in capital cities.

In order to exercise control, representatives have come together and developed the ***Party System*** which works well where central control is required (the party whip) but risks failing those constituents whose needs fall outside the perceived scope of the party itself.

In electing a party, the voter buys a *package manifesto* which provides priorities on a national basis and, in so doing, rides roughshod over the needs of the individual constituencies. It appears that the more distant the constituency is from Westminster the less the requirements of the constituents are recognised and respected.

There are numerous examples where MPs have followed the whip and voted against the wishes of (or their promises made to) the constituents who elected them.

In the UK, with a cultural divide between North and South, there is a clear need for greater local representation in the North, ideally by Independent Candidates; but independent candidates are only very rarely elected because a good many people traditionally vote for a (safe?) party they think they know, however inadequate that party may be.

Where an Independent does succeed in becoming elected their Constituents' voices, needs and expectations are diluted to the point of ineffectiveness by the party system in Westminster.

The party system gives structure and discipline, allows priorities to be set and has the collective weight to tackle the bigger issues – international trade, building warships and co-ordinated intelligence.

The independent system gives much stronger local representation, gives the electorate a genuine voice and presence and recognises local needs and priorities, but is overwhelmed by the party in power.

Neither system works particularly well.

If the independents could be co-ordinated in defined geographical areas away from the capital city they could speak more clearly for the particular needs of the people of their own areas and, given sufficient numbers, could actually influence and redirect government attention to their bigger local issues.

The argument below develops this case, using Yorkshire as a specific geographic area with its own culture, particular needs and a history of neglect from centralised party politics.

<u>The Case for Yorkshire</u>

Yorkshire represents a significant part of the UK by population and by area. We have our own culture and a history of neglect from Whitehall. It is a distinct region that can draw people together with a common purpose to improve their lives.

By co-ordinating independent candidates around a common purpose, the needs of the individual areas can be properly served whilst the more pervasive and bigger needs of the county as a whole can be collectively addressed.

Politicians, and governments, are notoriously weak with defining common, and lasting, purpose – attention is focused on themselves and the near-future (policy can be changed at a whim, strategy is lasting and delivers sustainable benefits. See below).

Yet, the one independent MP, acting alone, can only deliver benefits appropriate to a small area, cannot control the financial income that is derived centrally and has little input with the bigger issues.

There is a case to develop a constitution that is small enough to be relevant and large enough to have some clout in Westminster but sits within the established constitution.

A constitution within a constitution is developed more fully later, suffice it to say that there will need to be a co-ordination centre which the Independent MPs can subscribe to, or not. The challenge is to make this centre sufficiently relevant – by being the custodian of the common purpose with the policies and strategies that will deliver against this common purpose. And with an optimum of administrative support.

A Common Purpose

Government has but two reasons to be in existence:

- To defend the realm.
- To improve the lot of the people within the realm.

For the purpose of the argument, Yorkshire may be taken as *The Realm.*

And, there is a need for significant change; the scandals that emerged several years ago in *The Daily Telegraph* with examples of (unprosecuted) duck houses, chandeliers and subscriptions to porn sites highlighted how far our MPs had moved from the common purpose, and stories of self-interest still keep arising.

Current Lack of Common Purpose.

There have been break-away parties such as the *Gang of Seven* in February 2019 (Change UK) which was heralded with much sound and fury, yet signified nothing – their stance was effectively a negative one and without a defined purpose it sank within weeks.

Faring better was the SDP which established as a breakaway party in the early 1980s and formed a coalition with the Liberals a little later as a means to further their aims of positively uniting family, community and nation – working co-operatively with business to mutual benefit.

The SDP continues to hang on in there when other parties and break-away groups which have lacked clarity, or subscribed to a single aim (UKIP,

Brexit etc.), have served their short-term purpose and are now disassembling.

Our aim

To be financially self-sufficient to a point where we can enrich the lives of the people of Yorkshire; not just financially but also in terms of equality, community and opportunity. We can do this by preferentially supporting infrastructure and enterprise that adds real value – not the notional value associated with stocks, insurance or artwork.

Delivering Common Benefits

Improving the lot of the people within the realm involves the delivery of benefits – and people buy (vote for) benefits; the nature of which is developed at some length elsewhere[23]; however, in summary:

People generally subscribe to intangible benefits (quality of life) – things that deliver confidence, reassurance and peace of mind, more than they subscribe to tangible benefits – save, increase or reduce something, usually money related.

It is this confidence, reassurance and peace of mind that supports the party system – even if the party is rubbish, you know what you're getting and there is little in the way of uncertainty. The YDP will need to work hard to build this 'brand presence'.

Business tends to be the opposite – focusing on delivering tangible benefits (dividends and share

---

[23] See Beyond Money – a Guide for Sustainable Business; pp. 230-237.

price) to shareholders, and some times with scant regard for their workforce, pension funds or the aspirations of the community they operate in.

In a properly balanced constituency, both types of benefit have to be recognised and served through appropriate and fundamental strategies with policies developed accordingly (see *A Common Purpose* above); these strategies will remain true to the county whatever the external events or constraints[24].

The policies and manifestos may be treated more like the tactics required to get the job done.

What these are and how these will be achieved is developed later with regard to the community whilst respecting the need for industry to deliver profits to shareholders and at the same time respecting the needs and aspirations of its workforce and the community within which it operates.

The shape of Yorkshire Independence

The proposed structure of the Yorkshire Democratic Party might be considered to be a bit like the SDP but stopping at the level of the community and breaking away from national (London) control which is too blunt an instrument.

Integrating the Independents and recognising industry and society (see *Benefits* above) the

---

[24] Policies change often, depending on external events. Purpose (the Mission) stays constant whatever the external environment.

elected representatives can more fully encompass society in providing direction and draw the three elements (people, government and industry) together into a *Sweet-spot* (see appendix 4) that promotes mutual progress for all those involved.

Critical Mass

An analysis of substantial votes in the Commons (omitting votes on amendments) in 2019 indicated that 8 out of 19 key decisions have been won or lost by less than 40 votes i.e. 20 MPs voting differently would have changed the result.

In the medium-term. the aim of Yorkshire independence (from Whitehall) has to be to get to a critical mass of more than 20 seats; 30% of the total county vote; enough to be a thorn in Westminster's side or enough to encourage them to support our independence.

This is a model that could be adopted by other discrete, or 'fabricated', communities of adequate size and common mind-set e.g. Cockney, Geordie or Cornish. It would be up to them to adopt this, or a similar, model if they saw fit to do so.

Centralised Politics and Progress

Only the mediocre are always at their best.

J Giradoux

The party system needs a significant bureaucracy to ensure compliance by members, with established rules to provide discipline. The upshot of this is that change and progress is painfully slow and there is a zone of safety where the status quo is actively maintained and fought for (the earlier oxymoron – aggressive mediocrity).

It can be argued that this is one of the drivers of mistrust in politicians where within this safety zone there is no scope for error and a requirement by the party for infallibility. In business if you get 60% of decisions right, you're doing OK; the very least in politics is 100% otherwise you are undermining your own position within the party; safer to aim low and hit, instead of aiming high and risk falling short.

Probably the closest any politician came to admitting a mistake was over the eggs fiasco of several years ago then [paraphrased] *'I thought I made a mistake, but I was wrong'*.

This adherence to establishment with a regulated and cosy existence seems to have led to a regime of 'more of the same' and a loss of focus as to the purpose of being in Westminster beyond supporting the party that pays quite handsomely – providing the MPs with privilege but little responsibility.

The Purpose of Government?

Having asked this question of a number of politicians and people associated with politics, none seem to have a coherent answer. In arguing for an independent Yorkshire, the following basic principles may be used as a foundation for the policy that will inform strategy.

As noted earlier (and with no apologies for repetition) the fundamental purpose of government at any level is:

- To maintain the safety and integrity of the realm.
- To improve the lot of everyone within that realm.

Those two principles should cover the majority of government activity, yet seem to have been lost in the scramble for 'me first' and nest-feathering.

One aspect in particular that could lead to complications is that of defence. Today, maintaining nation safety is too big even for one country – including America; this aspect must be collectively managed and an independent Yorkshire will expect to deliver its contribution, both technically and with trained personnel.

As to improving peoples' lot, we do not do that by importing Chinese tat, neither do we improve peoples' lot by selling insurance and hamburgers to one another. We improve their lot by making and exporting quality goods and services (with real added value) in order to generate foreign currency that can be re-invested in the community.

And as to policy

It seems that if we have a policy (or a manifesto for that matter) politicians believe everything will flow; industry can invest and planning for the future is a little more certain. Very wrong …

For example, we once had a policy to curtail smoking in public places that originally included open spaces until one politician commented that after the birth of a child it would be unreasonable not to be able to relax in the local park with a small cheroot to celebrate – policy amended.

As to manifestos, Tony Blair had some twenty-one promised deliverables and achieved but two; Ed Miliband had five promises carved in stone, none were delivered, but we all had a good chuckle.

To improve peoples' lot there has to be clear planning and certain commitment, two things that require vision and purpose. It appears that vision is, at best, eighteen months before planning for the next election and commitment lasts until someone thinks of something better.

A Digression

It has been my privilege to work on several government programmes as well as being a trustee (short-term) for a regional initiative which was being relinquished by the County Council to be run by the community.

This latter initiative was perhaps one of the most salutary, in being headed by a career politician who was supported by senior people from the Council.

The business plan was pitiful, the cash flow unintelligible and of purpose there was none.

As a fairly urgent starter I produced a workable cash flow and was beginning to tackle the business plan to give direction and ultimately purpose in order to pitch for grants and planning applications.

On three occasions I asked the other trustees quite definitely (and a few promptings between) to define the purpose of the new venture. Even with this level of help and encouragement they were unable to produce anything meaningful, on the basis that *they had never done anything like this before*, which included the business plan and cashflow.

I resigned.

Impact of Party Discipline on Yorkshire

This lack of vision with an inability to define a meaningful future is all-pervading; to the point where we currently have:

Promises of infrastructure upgrades (e.g. A64 widening) going back more than 40 years and are still undelivered,

An MP who ignored several hundreds of villagers to promote a project and party line with just tens of followers – mostly based in Westminster, and

Flood management where significant damage was done, little was actioned for a good long time despite promises, and several years taken to replace critical bridges and roads – Tadcaster being just one high profile example. There is still severe flooding in the Dales whenever we get a decent storm. More recently, Snaith was devastated when the Aire, the Dales catchment run-off, burst its banks and put a flood plain under more water than ever seen before.

In order to provide a responsible plan, there is a simple five-step process which may be adopted by commercial enterprise but never (in my experience) by the public sector. Normally it's just more of the same, however pointless, repetitive and wasteful.

That simple process may be articulated as:

- Vision – what will it look (and feel) like when it comes together (may never be reached),
- Mission – what is the fundamental purpose,
- Objective – an outcome that is Specific, Measurable, Achievable, Realistic and Time-bound (SMART),
- Strategy – the route to achieving the objective,
- Tactics – the short-term actions that support the strategy, or put it back on course.

There is little like this in the public sector; but then, it's all about nice safe well-paid jobs so why change anything? See the note above about the regional initiative.

Creating Yorkshire's Road-map

In giving structure to the party and the basis for its development, the argument follows this well-rehearsed commercial journey:

Our Vision

For Yorkshire to be completely independent, solvent and self-governing with our own constitution.

Our Mission

To sit on top of England.

Our Objectives

(Still to be made SMART!)

- To maintain the integrity & safety of the county.

- To continually enrich the lives of the people of Yorkshire, not just financially but also in terms of equality, health, community and opportunity.

Our Strategy Summarised

Maintaining the integrity of the county is an activity that demands independence – or a good deal of the machinery for independence to be in place.

Some of the obligations are covered later and will be significant when the county is self-ruling. This is a long-term project that will unfold more fully once we have a degree of autonomy.

Meantime, as an integral part of the UK, the county will continue to play a part in defence (e.g. Catterick, Fylingdales, Linton-on-Ouse) and support the borders, the sea ports and the airports.

By supporting enterprise that adds real value, not the notional value associated with stocks, insurance or artwork.

Where restoring selected public ownership is involved this should happen with a minimum of resistance.

Ultimately, the aim is to be financially self-sufficient and able to meet all social responsibilities which includes amongst others: health, education, emergency services, infrastructure, environment, flood defence, sanitation and policing.

If each representative were truly independent, anarchy would ensue with a divided and weak voice that would not have the clout in the early days to persuade Westminster to provide adequate support.

To bring about these objectives there should be a loose union of Independent Parliamentarians with a central reference point that will ensure the county is represented as a whole and with a common voice that is stronger than its component parts.

In time, the level of representation will grow to a point where the county will be best served by a local majority party of its own making.

Being Yorkshire, we will not support wasters but will encourage and protect the vulnerable; neither will we sanction an administration bigger or more complex that is actually needed to run the county – and we do like to get our money's worth.

Tactics – a note

How things are manoeuvred on the journey to help reach the goal. In politics I believe that tactics pretty much equate to **Policies** which seem to be no more than expedient promises to get someone on side and, once on side, forgotten or replaced with something else more interesting.

A Modified Form of Governance

Currently in the UK there is a strong bias to the banks, the media and the public schools who's alumni control much of the financial sector and the media; there is too much self-interest to expect much to change with the party systems where control and self-interest is inextricably entwined in these institutions and those brought up in them.

A semi-feudal style constitution (loosely based on the island of Sark) provides a workable option, given a change in mind-set of the elected representatives.

A change in mind-set

England presents a singular phenomenon of an honest people whose constitution, from its nature, must render their government forever dishonest.

THOMAS JEFFERSON: *Letter to James Ronaldson 1810.*

Politics has, over the last fifty or so years, become ever more the province of the bullying narcissist with control in the hands of the very few – little different from medieval times where the monarch or local landowner had absolute power – one of the most worrying activities for a Prime Minister is a referendum because referenda hand over to *Direct Democracy* and cede power to the people.

By adopting an inclusive mind-set, control can be shared between a central function and the people being better represented with that central function managing the bigger (county-wide) issues and the electorate identifying which of those issues should have local priority.

However, this demands a different mind-set; one which I have not found in any psychometric – to work for others (altruistic) rather than to work for self.

The concept of co-operation needs to be there as well as the concept of competition – first is first, second is nowhere – fine on the sporting field but occasionally in society someone else's needs must take priority over yours and the disadvantaged need to be supported.

If we are to rise up and tackle both poverty and inequality, we need both altruism and co-operation to make any inroads – something rare today in government, and which might explain the position we are now in.

This concern for others will also help remove the idea that GDP is an end in itself which will, in turn, lessen the barriers to tackling climate change at a more fundamental level.

Decision-Making

Government promises – easily made, yet rarely delivered – why?

A decision involves commitment, and if held off for long enough, any decision becomes a good one[25].

To a competent manager the main purpose of a decision is to make the problem smaller; to a politician, focused on appearance rather than reality, the purpose of a decision is to push the eventuality into the distance, so that it just looks smaller (or gets lost in complications).

The major outputs are announcements that sound good but never lead anywhere. Some incisive

---

[25] Please see my paper in _The International Journal of Management and Decision Making._

decision-making would be a welcome change from today's pervasive dither and spin.

Measure What Matters, Not Everything
Decide what is actually important for the nation – not for the vanity of the few. As an example, a well-known confectionery company manages a global business on <u>just one financial ratio</u>; a government run Business Link reported 192 different variables on a monthly basis – bureaucracy gone mad. The confectionery company turns over billions of dollars a year, the Business Link a few million pounds.

This global business has a simple dictum – if administration is less than 16%, or more than 25% of income ***in any organisation*** they risk being ripped off (less than 16%) or they have no clear focus on where they're going (more than 25%) and they need to seriously revisit objectives and strategy.

As is the case in much of the public sector.

Reduce the Central Admin Function
As noted earlier, central government spends 43% of GDP on running costs, staff and admin; roughly twice what is needed to manage efficiently. The excess cost (at 10% of GDP) equates to about £200bn; for Yorkshire that would be 8.5% of £200bn or £16bn.

This is a mind-set that needs to be addressed, and could be started by Councils adopting zero based budgeting.

We are overburdened by red tape, obfuscation, measurement and blame[26]. So why not ***pension off the Mandarins*** who believe power comes with size of budget and numbers employed?

The impact would be to remove the protective cloak from the people below the mandarins, in turn opening the way for a proportion (the mediocre?) to be removed or redeployed.

A proportion of these are the people who, after 40 years of being paid well and given index-linked pensions will have contributed little positive or constructive to the benefit of society.

To pay them, Jobseekers allowance will no doubt be cheaper in the long run than the pay and pensions for the rest of their time in office.

The overall drive is to develop an economy that adds real value (not the imaginary value from financial instruments that can be wiped out at a stroke). Those well-trained public-sector workers, who choose to do so, can gain real satisfaction and also contribute positively to the development of the county by moving to the commercial sector.

Surplus budget could be reallocated as a welcome (and necessary) addition to other coffers or redeployed to worthwhile projects such as social housing, to alleviate poverty or address inequality.

---

[26] See Parkinson's Law.

A note about VAT

VAT was introduced to pay for running Europe, now with Europe gone VAT may be used to support local administration. Where efficiencies are introduced and the running costs come down VAT will be adjusted accordingly.

It is unlikely that VAT will be completely abolished but it will serve as a lasting inducement to people to demand value for money from their representatives.

Not quite comparing apples with apples: Lord Digby Jones[27] wrote in 2011 that in the past 40 years only eighteen teachers had been dismissed for incompetence, yet at the same time there were some 17,000 of them struggling; supported by OFSTED's figure of 15,000 failing teachers in 1995.

The average churn in the commercial world in 2016 is cited as 16% per annum[28] – a very significant difference, and one that should be considered with regard to the public sector.

A more focused system would create greater churn in the public sector, with increased efficiencies and with genuine talent appropriately applied and appropriately rewarded.

This increased efficiency should support a significant reduction in VAT; but a reduction that will no doubt only be recognised with

---

[27] Fixing Britain pg.135.

[28] SHRM 2017 Human Capital Benchmarking Report.

independence. Whitehall will no doubt continue to be profligate and mediocre.

Getting the vote

Background

It has long been stablished that people vote for a party with a package where a limited set of principles sits above, and are used to frame, the various policies for people who have made up their minds long before election day.

People will vote for an established party, however incompetent the person standing might be, so we need to establish the party and its principles.

For example, the Conservatives favour free-market economics with limited regulation and little opposition to the limits of personal progress whether financial or otherwise. The party supports defence.

There is an affiliation with the Commonwealth and an opposition to Irish reunification, or independence for Wales or Scotland; the party is largely ambivalent to membership (or not) of Europe.

The Labour party, on the other hand supports state intervention, greater equality for the members of society (with more even distribution of wealth) and greater rights for the workforce – but within the workings of a capitalist society. The party would lessen the defence capability.

There is an affiliation with Europe (included in the Party of European Socialists and the Progressive Alliance) with semi-autonomous branches in Wales and Scotland and whilst not contesting elections in Northern Ireland it supports the SDLP.

In more recent times, other parties have come and gone I suspect because: their message was not very clear, they formed on a negative footing – to protest about something each member personally disagreed with, rather than to deliver something positive collectively – and didn't get much traction with the media; beyond the news that they had been established; there was little genuinely newsworthy or of 'social interest' to nurture and develop.

Size of the Yorkshire government

Based on the Westminster set-up, there are approximately 650 MPs for the UK with, on average, one MP for each 91,000 of population (2011). Translated to Yorkshire, this would demand a representation of 60 MPs.

Constituency boundaries might be established using the main roads and railways as backbones to the various constituencies not as their borders. The boundaries come from rivers, mountains and the sea.

The Westminster Upper House is recommended to be reduced to under 600 members – just about balancing the Commons.

The need for an 'Upper House' is debatable and may be replaced with nine members: three from each riding and with terms of three years, staggered by a year. These may be drawn from past

Independent Candidates who have felt strongly enough to spend their own money on trying to improve on the party system that is the unsatisfactory state of our current government (unusually, I'm not looking for a job).

A Constitution Within a Constitution

Yorkshire is a county of contrasts with three of the UKs largest cities:

- Leeds – 774,000, third largest,
- Sheffield – 570,000, fifth largest,
- Bradford – 531,000, sixth largest.

And also, some of the most sparsely populated areas:

- The North York Moors,
- The Yorkshire Dales,
- The Yorkshire Wolds.

The requirements of these areas are very different which should be reflected in their governance, where party politics is not appropriate and independent representation is more suitable, in that the specific requirements can be tackled at the point of most need.

There is the opportunity to create different interest groups from the constituencies e.g. Rural for Pickering and Ripon, Cultural for York and Whitby or Industrial for Leeds and Sheffield. These would depend on the outcomes of the various elections.

The constituencies do not need to represent equal numbers of people because there is no vying for party supremacy or advantage; The city's representatives can represent a large number of people but not much physical area, whilst the rural communities will have fewer people but a larger area to represent.

Morals and Principles

The nature of the Yorkshire mind-set and the things that matter are addressed above; in developing the overlying package for the manifesto, these traits and requirements are summarised as:

- To ensure everybody has a fair chance in health and education.
- To be able to retain within the county the earnings created from our own endeavour.
- To be free to explore (invent, create, experiment) provided no-one is disadvantaged as a result.
- To give support to ethical industry.
- To ensure infrastructure properly supports people and business.
- To have business contribute a fair share to support the continual improvement of the community.
- To live and work in a safe environment.
- To respect nature & foster the legacy for our descendants.

The dynamics of the basic morals and principles may be described diagrammatically by:

The Big Picture – Things Working Together.

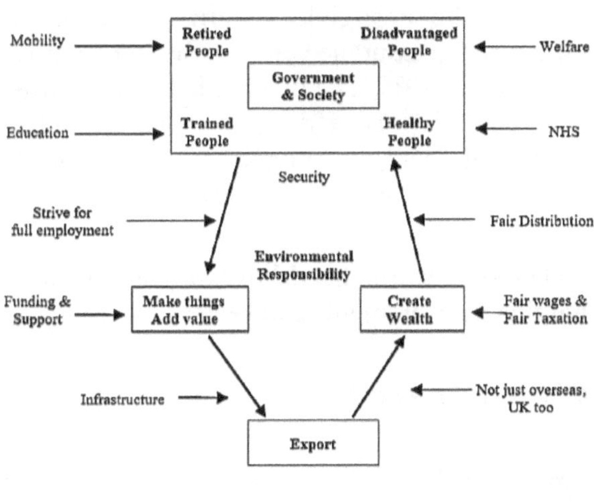

These principles support a truly integrated county but, to work well, the divisions between public and private ownership need to be developed more clearly.

One of the most damaging management mantras of recent times has been:

"If you can't measure it, you can't manage it"

This has set whole departments off to measure difficult things like toothache, irritation at being late for work, or overcrowding on the train.

Many years ago, a gentleman named Gronroos found that people (<u>not</u> government or industry) buy things mainly for their intangible benefits – what they do emotionally, not what can be measured.

This decision-making ratio has the big driver for people as the intangible benefit (peace of mind, confidence, reassurance etc – the unquantifiable stuff) – some 70%, The other side of the coin is the 30% tangible benefit (the big driver for governments and commerce, to: save, increase, reduce etc. – the quantifiable bit).

There's a warm handshake if you can tell me what this measurement represents:

$$VBTT = (1 - r - pq)MP + (1 - r)VW + rVL + MPF$$

Where *VBTT* is the value to business of travel time, r is the proportion of time saved allocated to leisure, p is the proportion of time that would have been spent working rather than travelling, q is the productivity whilst travelling relative to workplace productivity. *MP* is the Marginal Productivity of Labour, *VW* is the employees' valuation of work time respective to travel time, *VL* is the employees' valuation of leisure time with respect to travel time, and finally *MPF* is the value of additional output that arises from reduced travel time. ***The government's own analysis ignores a number of these factors.*** [my emphasis][29].

---

[29] It's the 'maths' for HS2, taken verbatim from the government publication.

For many of these unmeasurables, the solution has to be to take the service back into public ownership and allow them to be worked on with simple and obvious solutions and not to have the need to demonstrate measurable progress for the benefits of spin or the newspapers.

Some time ago, in order to make public finances look good (as measured in the public balance sheet for example) the Public Private Partnership (PPP) was invented, ostensibly to bring private sector skill into public sector management (when such expertise is readily hired). In reality, all this has done has moved an asset off the government balance sheet (making the ratios look better) and saddling the tax-payer with a significant long-term debt (effectively a rent).

Such enterprises need to be made wholly public or wholly private – there is no cost-efficient and manageable half-way house.

Another initiative that can sit alongside the PPP is making services like health 'competitive'. Instead of pretending to deliver 'better value' (whatever that is) such services could be brought back into public ownership and with their management commercially trained.

The overarching principles, developed below, take into account this pretence at measuring and delivering better value in order to create a stable but progressive county.

Integrated Party Principles

The four key stages (the engine)

As shown in the diagram above, a **healthy society** is self-supporting (more of this later) and will be more than capable of producing things that add real value.

The capacity to make things and **add tangible value** is an activity in its own right and also encompasses the capacity to grow things and mine things.

Having made, grown or mined things and added value to them, these things need to be exported. For a major company **export** can be to another country for the SME export might be considered over the county boundary and for a specialist or one-man-band export could be considered as the next town.

After adding and exporting value, that value has to be realised in the form of a payment that goes back to the value producer for equitable distribution, which includes the **tax** to keep this engine turning.

The linkages (the oil)

In order to add value, there need to be appropriate facilities, whether a factory or a desk, finance to support enlargement, attitude, skills and experience to support innovation, and expertise that supports continued, controlled growth.

A key consideration (not well-enough represented in the north) is an infrastructure that supports the community and its industry, whether getting people to work, goods to port or raw materials to factories.

Waterways and air transport can be considered along with roads and rail as means to move things or people as well as leisure opportunities (canal boats or flying off to exotic locations).

All the elements need to be able to operate safely and securely; police and judiciary need to be adequate and appropriately configured to be able to manage both urban and rural situations.

And (no doubt with some protests e.g. frackers?) this all has to happen in an environmentally responsible manner without fudging the issue by imaginary schemes such as carbon off-sets.

The diagram above links these principles into a dynamic and holistic approach which is self-contained and respects the environment as well as people, government and industry; it forms the basis for dynamic governance and appropriate investment.

The Manifesto

<u>Things that need to be tackled</u>

This is quite a long wish-list and not necessarily consistent with the UK as a whole or even between different parts of the county.

The order below may change by area, for example the coast needs better road access, the towns need better police and security.

- Infrastructure – needs urgent attention:
  - Rail is inadequate for the population and is unreliable,
  - Antique rolling stock on railways and the metros needs replacing,
  - Major roads are inadequate with coastal towns hard to access and goods slow to be transported,
  - Country roads – villages difficult to reach, isolation for the old and infirm,
  - High, and growing transport density – a properly integrated plan is needed.

- Appropriate education and training:
  - Industry,
  - Services e.g. health, security etc.

- Physical Health:
  - Short-term e.g. broken bones, colds,
  - Long-term e.g. diabetes, cancer,
  - Specifics e.g. dentistry,
  - Drugs and medicines – recreational, curative,
  - Old Age – home care, residential, palliative.

- Mental Health:
  - Curable e.g. increasing drug use, eating disorders, upbringing,
  - Incurable e.g. congenital.

- Social welfare that should be appropriate to need:
  - Fewer food banks and reduction of poverty,
  - Social security & housing.

- Support for agriculture and industry:
  - Financial – seasonal, long-term, short-term,
  - Technical – managerial, innovative, sales.

- Security and peace of mind:
  - Theft and low detection from rural areas,
  - Increasing threat levels in towns and villages,
  - Recreational drugs.

- Administration.

- National Parks & AONB:
  - Responsible tourism,
  - Repeal DEFRA's building recommendations.

- Climate change – it hasn't stopped raining:
  - Fracking,
  - Water management, flooding,
  - Renewable energy – wind, waves, sun etc.

- Service infrastructure:
  - Old gas, water & sewerage mains,
  - Internet, cabling, fibre-optics.

And Some Estimates of Cost

Infrastructure

Rail maintenance – government support £3.4bn across the UK. 8% of £3.4bn represents £275m [the rest comes from passenger fares]. This figure does not represent vanity projects such as HS2. <u>Additional funding would be required for better rail connectivity around the county.</u>

- Metro for Leeds (Est £100m per annum).
- A64 still needs to be addressed (£100m estimate).
- Other main road updates (based on the A64) – £150m.
- Road maintenance £50m p.a.
- Country lanes and by-ways (est. £25m p.a.).

Bus services between the larger towns and cities run at a profit and will continue to do so; however, between the towns and villages, buses make a loss.

A fourth form of subsidised transport needs to be introduced in addition to private cars, trains and buses; this is proposed to be a taxi-style service that runs out of the towns between villages and can be called by phone, computer or app, can be hailed (as is a Hackney Carriage, despite the rules) and can carry passengers on its return to a start point; there will be little need for a return to a taxi rank between journeys.

Because much of the journey will be paid by the fare the main costs will be in setting up an infrastructure and some subsidisation. Perhaps even invite Uber or a similar firm (why not?), but with some revised agreements about what constitutes a driver's territory.

Allow £10m – average £1m for the areas around the ten most appropriate towns and cities in Yorkshire.

Rivers & Canals to be developed and used to transport freight as well as encouraging leisure activities. (est. £10m maximum).

Total cost of infrastructure: £720m.

Education & Training

(using data from fullfact.org).

Assume population break-down is consistent across the UK; Yorkshire has 8.2% of the population and the education budget for the UK is £90bn (ONS).

The fair equivalent share appropriate to Yorkshire is £7.4 bn.

Physical Health

The UK spends £115bn on health. Of that:

- 63% is GPs and hospitals,
- 15% long-term care,
- 10% drugs outside of hospitals,
- 5% preventative healthcare,
- 3% other things.

Assuming <u>equal</u> apportionment across the UK:

Yorkshire should spend £9.4bn.

There should be a case for dentistry to be put back into the NHS to reduce sick days and, it is believed, dementia which is supposed to be initiated by poor oral health.

Hospices would be included early on; currently they are charitable with the uncertainty this brings.

Mental Health

Mental health encompasses a very wide range of ailments and symptoms. The UK spend on mental health is c.£17bn, but by rights should be £24bn. **For Yorkshire this represents £2.0bn.**

Welfare spending

Parliament has asked us to focus on how much the Government spends, not how well it spends it [OBR].

- State pensions amount to £92bn,
- Personal tax credits were £27bn,
- Housing benefit £23bn,
- Disability benefit £17bn,
- Incapacity benefit £15bn,
- Child benefit £12bn,
- Pension credit £6bn,
- Jobseekers allowance £2bn,
- Other £24bn,

The total cost to the UK is some **£217bn.**

However, this has been a very wasteful department [OBR note] plus £15bn (and rising) spent on the IT and management systems (please see the section about cabling and also Estonia).

Assume that a significantly more efficient system can be devised and the overall spend can be reduced by 20% to £174bn. Many claimants are underpaid and part of this saving will go to providing more adequate and appropriate allowances.

For Yorkshire, this should represent an annual spend of **£14.4bn.**

These proportions may be used in planning and assigning priorities.

The current UK system smacks of being devised by people who know the rules intimately – but have never played the game! But then, how could they, being on a salary of £80,000 plus perks plus other (sometimes substantial) income streams when the players themselves are on less than one tenth of this level of income.

There seems to be a case for seriously examining the systems in use and to consider scrapping or changing them to produce something better.

Support for agriculture

UK total spend on agriculture is about £5.8bn.

Yorkshire has a proportion of agriculture about consistent with our proportion of the UK population; however, with climate change and the likelihood of severe flooding becoming the norm there will need to be extra funding for soil preservation, reducing soil erosion and greater flood management. An extra 10% is added to the estimate equating to **support to the value of £0.55bn.**

Support for industry

The Department for Business Energy and Industrial Strategy directly supports UK industry etc. to the value of about £10bn a year.

An equivalence for Yorkshire of £1.0bn.

Security and peace of mind

The figure is put at 1.8% of UK GDP; the police account for 1%, the law courts 0.4%, prisons 0.2%, fire 0.1% and other services 0.1%.

The figure for Yorkshire equates to £3bn.

Administration

A figure of **£8bn** is derived elsewhere.

National Parks & AONB

Responsible tourism will act as a net cash generator and is considered under income – any costs will be offset by a greater net income.

In terms of policy, a recent report by DEFRA (Sept 2019) recommends building [sustainable small communities – my paraphrase[30]] on the national parks – despite empty properties in towns and brown land being available.

The likely ramification is a proliferation of holiday homes for those who don't need them but who could profit enormously from their later sale.

The cost of the upkeep of the parks is considered to be balanced by their income from tourism.

---

[30] Proposal 18 – see selected publications at the end.

Climate change

Renewable energy would be a net source of income. This would derive from tidal energy, wave energy, wind energy, sun and possibly hydro-electric.

Non-renewable energy will need to be phased out and this will be a project in its own right – balancing the income from renewables with the progressive cost of decommissioning existing power stations and the redeployment of staff. For the purpose of this thesis, energy is considered to be cost-neutral.

Water management and the sale of water outside the county are considered to be in balance; the income from the water sold being used to control flooding, water management and new reservoirs if appropriate.

Finance & climate change

As noted above GDP growth has become an end in itself and is no longer a means to an end; the reason being the continual need to prop up stock prices at almost any cost.

Yet stock prices are of interest to only about 15% of the population – the other 85% have no interest and suffer from this misguided focus under the constant media[31] coverage of 'the market' as if inequality is a good thing.

---

[31] Newspapers, television, radio etc. Each channel is a medium (plural *media*). Some have noted that a medium is neither rare nor well done.

Many of the quoted companies are energy intense and need to maintain levels of physical output to keep the profits flowing.

It is not in the interests of the wealthy to reduce profitability, now being achieved by any means – even 'hollowing out' once great companies and off-shoring profits to avoid tax, with the net result that the wealth gap is expanding.

There are two major impacts from this apparent need to keep stock prices rising:

- Energy usage continues to climb, but without investment in alternative forms of energy, so that profits are conserved (lack of investment, off-shoring) but greenhouse gases continue to be put into the atmosphere with the rich politicians pretending nothing is out of order (yet people choke and islanders drown whilst the oceans become more acidic, deoxygenated and increasingly polluted).

- In offshoring profits and avoiding tax (quite legal and preserves individual dividends and wealth) governments need to borrow increasing amounts of money to maintain the lifestyle their communities have got used to.

This additional money is simply printed by the banks (their balance sheets stay balanced as the debts are underwritten by imaginary government assets – remember Ponzi) and government debt

---

Some 50 or so years ago Michael Flanders (At the drop of a hat) pointed out that *Just enough happens every day to <u>exactly</u> fill all the newspapers* [my underline].

continues to grow whilst the planet continues to warm.

Service infrastructure

As with energy, this is considered to be cost-neutral; currently the costs of replacing old gas mains, old water & sewerage systems and some electrics are met by the profits enjoyed by the supply companies. There is no reason why this should change, whether in public or private hands.

Cabling, fibre-optics and other communication systems should be covered by the rental of their services. Some 'pump-priming' may be needed but against the overall cost, this is quite small and for the purpose of the argument are considered to be self-liquidating.

Not included

There is no case made for additional airport capacity; with three airports we should be self-sufficient for some time. The existing airports are within acceptable reach of most people.

Climate change through CO_2 emissions is also a major consideration and undermines the argument for airport expansion to a large extent.

Some Changes to Established Ways

Budgeting

The current ludicrous system demands departments 'spend up to budget' in order to have the same resources next year; coupled with notional power being vested in the size of a budget and the number of employees in the department this simply leads to huge wastage.

The initiative will be zero-based budgeting, where departments build their spending plans on actual documented need as projected for the year ahead. Vanity projects may be challenged and realistic local priorities established.

Drugs & Medication

There has been much in the press about expensive American drugs and NICE being hung out to dry with promises that the NHS will never be offered as part of a deal to the Americans – fair enough it needs investment and the assets are difficult to sell.

More to the point is the use of American drugs in the NHS, drugs that support the US pharmaceutical companies which fund the US government to an obscene level; the aim being to maintain the rise of American GDP at our expense. My guess is that the Americans would like to sell their drugs in the UK market at US prices, often ten times the price and in some cases 200 times the UK price[32].

The opportunities for greater use of generics e.g. from India should be re-examined and replacements used wherever possible; there are horror stories of aspirin costing 16p a pack in the supermarket and £8.50 in the pharmacy.

Many years ago, Professor David Nutt; the UK expert on drugs, recommended that a number of

---

[32] https://www.pharmaceutical-technology.com /features/us-most-expensive-drugs-uk-prices/

recreational drugs be cautiously legalised and made available from the pharmacy. The benefits from this initiative would include:

- Addicts getting the right preparation and not an untested compound cut with detergent, rat poison, talc or whatever. The sufferers could also be more readily contacted and treated.
- Some crime and prostitution is committed to obtain the money to support a habit in people who are too addicted to work, leading to break-ins and police attention.
- Other crime relates to 'turf wars' where the drug suppliers compete for 'customers' and increasing personal income.
- Child crime may also be linked to drug use and distribution; not a good start into a responsible adult life with potential problems later.

There is a case to be made to re-examine the legalisation of some recreational drugs and to explore potential sources of generic preparations[33], something we could do if we were independent.

---

[33] Cynics might well argue that, for the major pharmaceutical companies the cost of providing the cure is financially more lucrative than providing the fix. In the USA, parties and individual politicians have become very wealthy courtesy of the pharmaceutical companies. It is not part of vested self-interest to undermine their profits. There are many examples on Google for the US.

For a view of size, scale and influence, see also the House of Commons report on the impact of Brexit on pharmaceutical companies HC382 17/May/2018.

Commercial Finance

Provide positive support for business & agriculture by making allocated money directly available for borrowings and cash flow. An option would be to open the Post Office as a lending bank to give it a new lease of life and support the rural communities.

Much innovation is in the SME sector, but under-developed due to weak available funding – Dyson is an example, emigrating to Japan for support. Trevor Baylis (wind-up radio) is quite vitriolic about government's lack of understanding, weak support for innovation & ignorance of intellectual protection.

At the same time, it might put some pressure on the investment arms of the major banks to act responsibly for once.

Invention & Innovation

I argue we should support more invention and innovation at the SME level, much of the current support is tied to higher education (often slow and unaware of commercial confidentiality) or to big companies that can handle the weighty bureaucracy needed to administer a government grant.

To re-establish organisations like the Business Links could put genuine support where it is needed by people capable of delivering that support and also act as a centre to put people in touch with one another to improve their marketing and help to drive sales.

As with commercial finance the Post Office might readily act as a conduit for development funds and investment capital to entrepreneurs and inventors (considered too risky by the investment banks), supported and guided by the New Business Link's Personal Business Advisors.

Make Taxation Fairer

Big companies invoicing from tax-havens with minimal profits declared in the UK (Starbucks, Google etc.) and wealthy people with tax avoidance schemes. Precious little finds its way back into UK society by way of corporation tax or income tax.

Some people might argue that profitable companies would go abroad, but then if a company isn't paying the right tax in the UK, or is foreign owned (repatriating profits) is this an argument of any substance?

A similar argument exists with wealthy individuals: we are told we could lose them if tax regimes are unfavourable to them. But many of them are registered as non-domiciled (here for less than 150 days a year) and so <u>avoid</u> significant taxation. Another spurious argument?

In many instances individual wealth comes from company dividends and profits. This can be taken at source by the re-introduction of purchase tax.

As noted above, the avoidance of tax (however legal the method) is an avoidance of an obligation to support the societies that provide talent, labour and a market.

Connectedness for all

The internet is central to how things are done today; it has its disadvantages in that data is readily available, yet people take this as information, don't debate and forget to think or socialise. However, the benefits of connectivity are immense and also economically desirable.

Hull was connected by fibre optics over ten years ago and has continued to develop with advantages for business, local opportunities flagged and social benefits with access to services that can be discounted to residents; these services can include on-line learning, security, fitness etc.

The service is run by KCOM, a virtual monopoly and no doubt people are uneasy that 'big brother' is watching everything that they do, but 'Big Brother' is already keeping tabs on us, so no change there.

As an example, Estonia[34] is a fully digital country with UK MPs visiting from time to time to see how things are done. Interestingly, the team who set it all up ascribe their success to keeping the politicians completely out of the way and neutralising their ability to prevaricate and change the specification (see *Policy vs. Strategy* elsewhere).

Estonia has 1.4m actual residents and 10m virtual residents; the IT structure is kept safe by being a distributed system and significantly cheaper than traditional government – the whole package cost less than €100m; by comparison, just one UK project – Universal Credit (managed centrally) cost £15.8bn and is still rising.

So, relatively, it's not very expensive and Yorkshire already has a working template with Hull.

---

[34] See *Professional Manager* Spring 2019

<u>Manage Immigration</u>

Immigration is a very emotive subject and the UK is probably the only country in Europe without ID Cards. No-one overseas makes a fuss about having the means to identify themselves and most find it beneficial.

By the time there is sufficient momentum to properly implement the independent state, a number of things should be available including facial recognition that works (the DVLA already uses number plate recognition), interconnectedness and absolute clarity of purpose with education, industry and health directed to managing that state.

A points system based on overall strategic need can be readily developed and updated using the IT infrastructure, ID cards will include capabilities and people can be welcomed according to demographic and commercial priorities.

Currently (2020) for immigrants, there is talk of a minimum pay threshold in the region of £25,000; this would preclude people entering (the UK) for agricultural or hospitality work for example.

An option for such work; where Yorkshire has a high level of agriculture; might be a referral system where someone here proposes an individual and a second person endorses the proposal (a bit like a club) and if any one of them misbehaves, all three are fingerprinted, iris scanned and have their passports removed before being immediately deported to their home country[35]. Please see also the note on law and order below.

---

[35] We get numerous references to human rights; the argument here is that if a criminal has removed

Bannerjee and Duflo (see bibliography) argue from recent research that immigration is beneficial provided the immigrants stay within the boundaries of the country they move to – despite sending money home!

Sea Ports

There are a number of coastal ports and towns which can readily be developed into Free Trade Areas.

The actual status will be determined by the trading agreements in place at independence; whether a Free Port, a Nation State or something newly invented, the governance will be appropriate to Yorkshire and be a part of the larger legislature.

Airports

Highly polluting but make a sound contribution to the county's finances. They will not go away however much we protest. We have to be pragmatic and accept their presence, anticipate cleaner aircraft and fewer journeys (more use of IT & Connectivity).

Airport taxes, based on those currently levied will be maintained and contribute to the finances of the county. This is calculated below.

The argument to extend Heathrow and develop HS2 as a service to develop the north is hardly

---

someone's human rights (by robbing them or attacking them for example) in return, they will have their own human rights removed regardless of arguments about the degree of punishment or prejudice on their return home.

credible as it would add at least two hours to any incoming journey north.

Climate Change
No accident that this follows airports.

We do not inherit the earth from our ancestors, we borrow it from our children (variously attributed). A splendid example of today's politicians ignoring the experts.

There is a need to reduce climate change drivers (CO_2, methane etc.). As noted earlier clean energy will be encouraged, developed and exported – both as the energy itself and as the technology to generate energy.

There is also a case to be made for people to justify the use of airplanes for (essentially) local journeys e.g. to London when there is a perfectly acceptable rail service; the aim is to discourage short flights and reduce harmful emissions.

Properly managed, these initiatives will lead to potential income, reduce overall costs or point the way to reduce costs.

Joining the Dots – Implementation

<u>List of necessary activities</u>

A number of activities need to be brought together and sequenced in order to bring about the YDP. These are summarised here.

- Get together a core team of similarly minded individuals with experience of politics – both local and party.
- Finalise the structure and priorities for the party.
- Review and publish the manifesto and financials.
- Articulate the benefits to business and society of our being independent.
- Devise a selection procedure for potential representatives[36] and related to the benefits to be delivered.
- Select appropriate representatives.
- Start the funding process – businesses, wealthy donors, public subscriptions, crowdfunding etc.
- Establish and maintain extensive local publicity – Westminster will no doubt be concerned with the South-East for some time yet, so we can get on with it largely unimpeded.
- Ensure the publicity is capable of being ramped up six to nine months before the next election.

---

[36] The criteria will involve *works for others* as opposed to *works for self*, a spectrum that seems to be missed from all the main selection criteria and psychometric tests.

- Create the (secure) technology to link all the involved people together.
- Identify individuals who are photogenic, present well and articulate ideas convincingly.
- Get photogenic individuals on TV and in other visual media; the rest can go on the radio and social media.
- Get individuals out and about locally, addressing meetings with local concerns and (crucially) their solutions as would be delivered by the YDP.
- On the basis that at least 3-4 candidates will get elected start to ramp up the party profile.
- Lots of rallies and demands for independence (compare the SDP & learn from their approach).
- Support those in Parliament to be a thorn in the side of the elected majority, vociferous and critical; secure positions on influential committees and generate dialogue with those in Yorkshire.
- Begin the cycle again, apply the lessons learned and work towards independence with greater resolve, more MPs and a bigger following.
- Revise the manifesto, strategy etc. in the light of new learning and publicise the benefits widely.

Taxation & Income

Introduction

The notes below are illustrative of Yorkshire's self-sufficiency; over time the levels of taxation will change and opportunities to raise revenue will change. It is to be expected that these figures will, in time, be re-cast.

The purpose here is to demonstrate that there is actually the capacity to become self-sufficient.

Increasing GDP should be a means to an end and not the end in itself, as it has now become – increasing profits and dividends to be siphoned into the bank accounts of a wealthy few is a loss to the society that actually added the value to generate those profits in the first place.

Looking back, the Mill-owners behaved in a similar way – employing automation, where we now use connectivity, to drive down wages and increase margins[37] which fed their lavish life-styles.

Thankfully, the Trades Unions emerged and restored a bit of balance and sanity. The New Yorkshire will accommodate the needs of the population with a tax system that ensures appropriate tax is collected and that it is then used to benefit the community, not a small number of individuals.

---

[37] Over the years 1777 – 1853 the price for a piece of cloth (a week's wages for a handloom weaver) fell from £1.34, through 73p to 27p – this reduction in wage by 80% brought immeasurable distress to the working classes.

There are no easy answers to what appear to be easy questions – just throwing more money at it is not the solution.

Current government finance is based on paying the interest on borrowings against projected income, then next year borrowing again to pay the interest on last year's borrowings; and so the debt grows.

As noted earlier, this no more than a Ponzi scheme and there is a real risk it will all fall over.

Financially a system can be established that does not depend on borrowing and where expenditure is balanced by income. This is summarised below.

In this day and age, we need to consider the economics as a major part of the practicalities. The political posturing and ego-drivers can follow later.

The figures below are based on three assumptions:

- That production, sales and marketing will continue at the current level, or thereabouts,
- That levels of taxation and duties are pretty consistent throughout the UK,
- That the benefits and losses caused by exiting the EU will balance in time.

<u>The Barnett Formula</u> has been used for a long time to distribute money to the counties, even though Joel Barnett was embarrassed by it and said many times before he died that it was unsatisfactory[38], however it still forms the basis for

---

[38] The continuation with an unsatisfactory approach is typical of government (better the devil you know ...) and does not bode well for anyone wanting to influence economic

distribution and, as such, people have continued to work with it[39].

Potential Savings

As noted above, in Reduce the Central Admin Function and taking central government as representative (this can be challenged) they spend 43% of GDP on running costs, staff and admin; roughly twice the ratio that is spent by NYCC; the Yorkshire administration will not need to prop up an Upper Chamber or overseas interests.

There will be savings by not drawing funds to finance HS2, the House of Lords or the No.3 runway at Heathrow to name some of the current initiatives.

Armed services are not considered because in this day and age defence is more than one nation can manage on its own. There is a quid-pro-quo argument that we can pay our share and provide an appropriate proportion of personnel through Catterick for example, renting Fylingdales or leasing the Leeds barracks and training schools.

Target Income

According to the Barnett formula public spending per head in 2015/16 for Yorkshire & Humberside

---

thinking e.g. Steve Keen and others – so no change before the whole sorry edifice falls over.

[39] It seems to be based on per capita support when surely a more equitable algorithm would have per capita as the main part but tempered with a calculation for population density (we need roads etc.) which is based on area – a squared function and therefore a much greater impact than just per capita.

was £8,791. On this basis and with 5.3m people in the county this indicates £45bn to run things.

£44bn represents 8% of the total UK tax take – the proportion of the population in the county.

Government stats put the figure for 2015/16 at £47,389m (£47.4bn) – so the assumption looks right to within ± 5%.

Raising our own taxes could generate c.£46bn before exploring the sale of goods and services to neighbouring counties e.g. water & electricity to Lancashire, Cumbria and Northumberland.

A note about technology

Technology continues to advance and people continue to take advantage of it. On the one hand there is the increasing control and accuracy noted above under *Borders and Boundaries* and on the other hand is the increased connectivity and personal convenience.

Connectivity can enhance and simplify local administration (see VAT above) whilst increasing its effectiveness, people are more easily kept in touch and services easily rendered to outlying places.

Personal convenience will prompt, for example, on-line shopping which brings positives and negatives – dead town centres but access to a wider range of goods.

However, on the positive side, it will deliver two critical advantages for an independent Yorkshire.

The first is the ability to take purchase tax at point of sale (see below) and so avoid the tax avoidance schemes of the bigger companies, thus ensuring the social fabric of the county is supported and maintained.

The second advantage is to be able to compare prices and availabilities here and elsewhere (there are a plethora of comparison sites – Trivago, Go Compare etc.) so that, traders who artificially inflate their prices can have the inflated margin collected along with purchase tax to reduce cheating and perhaps provide a little extra income to society.

Similarly, EPOS sales and credit/debit card sales can also be monitored to ensure appropriate taxation is collected (Big Brother) at point of sale.

Sources of income

The sources noted below are based on current income streams of tax and duty; government has an ability to invent taxes as required[40] and this luxury must remain an option.

Initial calculations indicate that the following areas of activity can be readily monitored and appropriately taxed:

---

[40] Income tax was a temporary war measure, window tax resulted in bricked-up windows in some areas and loads of windows in stately homes, time was taxed and led to the *Act of Parliament* clocks; recently there has been bedroom tax and a growing upswell in interest in *Land Value Tax* which is unlikely to be popular in Yorkshire.

Community charge

The house prices are based on 1991 figures and therefore difficult to deal with. The mean community charge is about £1,750 – band D.

There are 2.222m households.

2.222 x 1750 = **£3.9bn** from community charge.

Purchase Tax replaces Corporation tax

Yorkshire households spend an average of £525 per week. Corporation tax at 2% represents:

525 x 52 x 2% = £550 per annum per household.

With 2.25m households in the county the domestic contribution would be £550 x 2,250,000 = £1.25bn.

The larger businesses reclaim VAT, although the smaller ones do not. To provide an estimate for sales through the non-VATable businesses a figure of £0.25bn has been added (without being justified in government statistics!).

Total corporation tax is estimated at **£1.5bn.**

Business Rates

Despite pleas to reduce business rates, the current situation is used for calculation.

York, North Yorkshire and the East Riding have:

  48,000 micro businesses (0-9 emps.) 53,000 units,

  4,800 Small businesses (10-49) 8,000 units,

  760 Medium businesses (50-249)1,420 units,

  160 Large businesses (250+) 150 units.

Based on c.45% of the rateable value of the property:

- East riding commercial property has a total rateable value of £250m[41],
- Leeds alone has a commercial rateable value of £850m.

Without tackling every town, city and riding (life's too short) here's an estimate:

- North & West Ridings outside the big cities: The East Riding is about 17% of the county and attracts £250m. This may be multiplied by six to give a county-wide estimate: <u>£1.5bn.</u>
- Big cities: Leeds, Sheffield, Bradford, Hull, Wakefield, – assume from £850m to £500m.
- Medium-sized cities and towns which includes: Huddersfield, York, Rotherham, Doncaster, Barnsley, Pickering, Scarborough, Dewsbury, Selby, Thirsk, Batley and others, assume £400m to £250m.
- Allow five additional big cities to 'mop up' the many medium-sized cities and towns.
- Three Ridings: £1,500m,
- five big cities (plus five)   £7,500m,
- Five medium town/cities   £1,500m.

Total business rates may be estimated at £10.5bn. This is taxed at a little over 45% as the cost to do business.

45% of £10.5bn would yield **<u>£4.7bn.</u>**

---

[41] E. Riding ref. (http://www2.eastriding.gov.uk/business/business-rates/freedom-of-information-requests-for-business-rates/) similar websites for other commercial areas.

Income tax, NI & personal taxation

Wages in Yorkshire vary between £28k in Leeds, through £26k in Bradford and York to £23k in Doncaster. For calculation an estimate of £26k is taken which is low when set against the national averages.

Maintaining income tax, NI and employers' NI at current rates, the tax take per individual will be a total of £7,215 per annum.

Nomisweb estimates that York, the North Riding and the East Riding have 583,000 economically active people, 60,000 economically inactive, c.60,000 who are sick or acting as carers and 26,000 who are retired. 12,000 people are claiming benefit.

Nomisweb estimate that Leeds City Region has:

1.5m people who are economically active, 61,000 unemployed and c.260,000 economically inactive. There are 153,000 workless households, 63,000 people claiming benefit and 75,000 people looking for a job.

Nomisweb estimate that for the Humber region 455,000 are economically active, c.100,000 are economically inactive and 30,000 are looking for a job, 67,000 are sick, carers etc., 18,000 are retired and 21,000 are claiming benefits.

The totals for recorded data are:

Economically active: 2,538,000

Others:

- Unemployed

 - Sick, carers etc.

- Retired

- Claiming benefits

Economically inactive: 620,000

The key data are (minor rounding):

Economically active: 2,540,000.

Economically inactive: 620,000.

Total: 3,160,000.

Not all areas are available in the Nomisweb data but another estimate indicates that 55% of the UK population are of working age. The population of Yorkshire is 5,450,130 people and 55% of this equates to 3,000,000 which is close to the figures from Nomisweb (3,160,000) and used to form the basis of the income calculation from personal taxation.

The economically active part of the population of Yorkshire earns an average £26,000 and pays £7,215 tax per person. Given 2,540,000 economically active persons (Nomisweb), this will realise **£18.33bn**.

VAT

Not all expenditure will be subject to VAT; the assumption (ass-u-me) with overall sales is that 50% will be from registered firms and the other 50% will be non-VATable products (e.g. childrens' clothes) and SMEs that are too small to register.

£88bn[42] x 20% x 50% (yes, I know you shouldn't multiply percentages) = £8.8bn; round to **£9.0bn** from VAT.

<u>As a check:</u>

Total UK VAT was £132bn.Yorkshire represents c.8% of total expenditure. £132bn. x.08 = <u>£10.56bn</u>.

Duties – fuel, alcohol etc.

Alcohol Duty

Alcohol duty is c.£25 per litre of pure alcohol in alcoholic drinks.

Average UK consumption is 12 litres of pure alcohol per person (15 - 65) per year (Wikipedia).

This equates to £300 per person per year in duty. Using this statistic gets rid of: men vs. women, beer vs. wine, teetotallers vs. drinkers.

76% of the Yorkshire population are of drinking age, or 5.4m x .76 = 4,100,000. At £300 per person, this will raise **£1.23bn** p.a.

Tobacco

The Office for National Statistics states that the average smoker gets through 11.3 cigarettes a day – say half a packet.

17.2% of the adult population smoke.

Using the statistic above of 4.1m adult people:

---

[42] VATable sales in Yorkshire.

In Yorkshire 17.2% of 4.1m = 700,000 people.

To allow for the impact of vaping and continuing decline, the duty on cigarettes is taken as a lower figure of £200 per 1,000 cigarettes, so a packet of 10 (average usage) would attract duty of £2.00 per pack.

Tobacco duty could raise £2.00 (duty per pack) x 700,000 (smokers) x 365 (days per year).
Tobacco duty could raise c.**£515m**.

Petrol and other fuels

UK fuel duties come to some £25.8bn in total; the proportion for Yorkshire would be £2.13bn; however, population density is low and public transport poor, for the purpose of estimation this is rounded up to **£2.5bn**. In time electric cars will be used more extensively and this duty will phase out.

Vehicle Excise duties

The total for the UK is £6.1bn; apportioning this for Yorkshire will yield **£504m**.

Pay your dues

Examples include paying for some services provided by the public sector e.g. hospital meals (I am cold and cruel – I hear you cry). Yet whilst in hospital, meals are provided and do not need to be paid for at home; it is logical to levy £20 per week to cover food costs or £3.00 per day). There were, in the UK, 16.5m hospital admissions in 2015/16. Average length of stay is about 5 days.

Yorkshire represents about 8% of the UK which calculates to 16.5m x 8% = 1.3m admissions, each requiring 5 days or an annual 'usage' of 6.5m days which would yield **£20m** per annum.

As an aside, if the total cost of a nurse is £40k per annum (pay, NI, uniform, etc.) this levy would pay for about 500 additional nurses just for Yorkshire.

Incoming retirees

A number of people move from the expensive south into Yorkshire and contribute no more to the local economy than the person who sold them the property they now live in.

There will be a financial premium applied to moves into the area, applied in much the same way as that in Jersey.

According to Plumplot.co.uk the average property price in Yorkshire is £187k; the average in England & Wales is £292k.

On average moving into the area releases c.£100,000 to the incomer. This may be taxed at 20% (comparable to corporation tax) to realise £20,000 per purchase.

The same source identifies 82,000 property sales in 2018/19 (November to November). If only 5% of these are people moving into the area, this represents a little over 4,000 taxable transactions or:

A net contribution of **£80m**.

Stamp Duty

Stamp duty for the UK is £13.5bn; apportioning this for Yorkshire should yield £1.12bn; but considering the average value of property is lower in Yorkshire this is reduced to **£900m**.

Air Passenger Duty

This is currently £26 per person on short-haul and £150 per person on long-haul.

There are three airports:

Leeds & Bradford	4m passengers,
Doncaster	1.5m passengers,
Humberside	0.5m passengers.

Assume only 20% are long haul, this would generate duties of:

Short haul 4.8m x £26 = £125m,

Long haul 1.2m x 150 = £225m,

Total revenue from Yorkshire airports; **£350m**.

Planning applications

North Yorkshire 2019 saw approximately 6,500 planning applications with a population of c.600,000 Translated across the county with 5.4m people this represents a total of 58,000 planning applications submitted.

The lowest council charge for a planning application is £206 which would yield **£12m** in a full year.

Minor and other taxes

These include:

Aggregates levy, climate change levy, landfill tax, betting & gaming, petroleum revenue tax, insurance premium tax, customs duties & levies, inheritance tax, capital gains tax and *other taxes and royalties*.

For the UK in total these add up to £32.4bn. The proportion appropriate to Yorkshire is slightly more than **£2.8bn**.

There has been interest in Land Value Tax since about 1915 when land values started to rise for the privileged few. This is a tax which keeps being considered and then put to one side for 'next time'.

Naturally, it will be resisted by the 'great and the good'[43] but would serve to redistribute income and reduce inequality. Perhaps later?

[43] Bedroom tax is OK because that only hits the little people and the disadvantaged.

<u>Income summary</u>

Current Income	£45,000m (Barnett).
Community Charge	£3,900m.
Purchase tax	£1,500m.
Business rates	£4,700m.
Personal taxation	£18,330m.
VAT	9,000m.
Alcohol duty	£1,230m.
Tobacco duty	£515m.
Fuel duty	£2,500m.
Vehicle Excise duty	£504m.
Pay your dues	£20m.
Incomers	£80m.
Stamp Duty	£900m.
Air passenger duty	£350m.
Planning applications	£12m.
Minor Taxes	£2,829m.

Income from local taxation: **£46,370m.**

This summary <u>omits</u> additional possibilities such as:

- Technology patents and intellectual protection of supported invention and innovation.
- Sale of water, electricity and other resources to different parts of the UK?
- Income from rail franchises?
- Land Value Tax.

<u>Expenditure Summary</u>

Infrastructure development & maintenance £720m.
Education   £7,400m.
Physical Health   £9,400m.
Mental Health   £2,000m.
Welfare   £14,400m.
Agriculture   £550m.
Industry support   £1,000m.
Security etc.   £3,000m.
Administration   £8,000m.

Total county expenditure: **£46,470m.**

The net 'deficit is c.£100m which will be made up from increased efficiencies, small surpluses and underspends from zero-based budgets.

We need to consider a number of possible social costs, not currently allowed for and may need additional revenue, or revenue redistribution. These include:

Insurance is notably slow to pay out – we still have people seeking money for their flooding a year and more after the event. This is iniquitous.

Likewise, with compensation – particularly the health service; I know a local woman who spent twelve years to get compensation for a damaged eye; she was on Legal Aid and the NHS paid the other side. Twelve years of lawyers' fees added up to quite a lot, with the government paying both sides.

Issues such as these need to be resolved.

In summary

The pages that follow serve to draw the strands together.

Now that it has been established that the Yorkshire Democratic Party is financially workable some of the points to consider are set out below:

Preamble

Over the next few years there will be turmoil as a number of international events play out, including:

- Our leaving the EU and misguided 'negotiations' aimed at enriching one side at the expense of the other with no thought of how to secure mutual benefits.
- Increasingly weird weather patterns which have (2019/20) caused flooding and crop failures with the probable consequential increases in food prices – and all the fault of the government! We can build on this likely discontent.
- The likely collapse of the dollar which will cause a world-wide recession and the various economic models to be re-thought.
- A world-wide downturn in trade brought about by a recognition of climate change and an acceptance that (in the western world) we already have enough 'stuff'.
- The impact of the Chinese 'flu still has to be felt and any 'aftershocks' still have to play out. This could find its way into the downturn in trade and other issues that this brings.

- Connectedness, with communication, and access to information (including eavesdropping) more readily available; this could cause a reduction in original thought (stupidification) as people access data (selected for them) and no longer challenge accepted wisdom (also referred to by some as *The Echo Chamber*).
- Religious wars – we're isolated from them in Yorkshire but there could be implications for trade and travel.
- Obesity coupled with living longer will stretch medical care and pensions.

More locally (UK specific) a number of initiatives will play out over the next four years with the following political impacts (my guesses):

- HS2 – delivering little of the proposed impact and causing general UK dissatisfaction at this waste of taxpayers' money and poor decision-making by the Conservatives (especially if the Chinese lay the rails and the Germans build the trains).
- Heathrow runway three – likely to cause significant environmental impact in the airport, surrounding areas and access points. There will be no direct benefit to the north; but nationally the protest groups and people of Harmondsworth and Southall will put a lot of pressure on, as will the people of Uxbridge and South Ruislip, generating more manifestos and policies that evidently cannot be delivered.
- Repairs and upgrades to the Palace of Westminster where MPs and the Lords will be re-housed somewhere a lot smarter than the

local businesspeople and residents could afford thus causing some resentment and more stark comparisons between north and south (York and London at the time of writing).

It's always easier to spend someone else's money.

Up to year four of the current government there will be a brief honeymoon to start and the north (Northern Powerhouse – whatever that is) will get a bit of attention, but that will soon dwindle as the vanity projects kick in again and their funding starts to drain the northern initiatives rather than cause disadvantage to Westminster.

From years four to five with an election due and a bunch of northern Conservatives (currently in safe Labour seats) now getting some traction there will be a brief flurry of activity to try to ensure the 2019 voting pattern is repeated.

So, we have a window of three and a half years (allowing for time to get this argument to market) in which to get a party together, raise funds and be sufficiently organised to cause voters from all parties to consider the Yorkshire Democratic Party a viable option and begin to open the door to central government and then to independence.

The steps outlined below are based on the objectives derived earlier and will take quite some time to accomplish; thankfully we have a number of years and the unfolding global events could well put the current government on the back-foot and open opportunities for Yorkshire independence.

You will note that there are no policy documents because (as stated earlier) a policy can be amended at a moment's notice (usually based on popularity polls) whilst a strategy is founded in purpose and objectives which do not change with time. HS2 is typical, every time there is a policy change the price goes up.

As if to justify a lack of strategy, there emerged around 2017 a cop-out for politicians disguised as VUCA (Volatile, Uncertain, Complex and Ambiguous) – a series of excuses as to why decisions were transitory. Either that or an attempt by a consultancy to drum up new business. This is summarised at Appendix 1.

Mindset

As noted earlier, in business, if you get 60% of decisions right there is every chance you will be very successful. The trick is to admit to the 40% that didn't go right and apply that learning in moving forward.

In today's established politics, once elected, you have to become infallible which usually means either hiding (or disguising) your mistake so no-one learns, taking collective decisions to hide responsibility or finding someone to blame.

The classic admission of an incorrect judgement runs along the lines *'I thought I made a mistake but I was wrong'*.

The impact of this lack of tolerance is that people get hurt (WASPI[44] Women, Universal Credit etc. etc.); surely, the simple thing to do is admit the error, recognise the real problem, resolve it and move on.

One feature of the Yorkshire psyche is a rejection of deceit; we have the backbone to be able to hold honest discussion without rancour and the strength of character to hold our hands up, put things right and even engage others who have better experience than we have.

Reducing Inequality

We need to clearly distinguish between poverty and inequality. Current government focus is on reducing poverty, often through a redistribution of personal taxation funnelled through the welfare system.

Inequality is quite different and based on historic economic thinking that there needs to be inflation and a continued rise in GDP otherwise, we are told, there will be recession and catastrophe.

As noted above, the growth in GDP should be a means to an end, not the end in itself which is the current focus and used to prop up the stock markets to ensure the wealthy stay wealthy whilst living standards for the rest of us decay, but not too slowly.

Elsewhere I refer to using the Post Office as an investment bank and a revised Business Link type activity to support and develop start-ups and work

---

[44] Women Against State Pension Inequality.

with the relatively unproductive companies to help turn them round.

The inescapable fact is that inequality is growing[45] and existing government policy does not address this. Current policy focuses on alleviating poverty – a very different thing.

This disparity is often hidden in ratios: for example, someone on £800,000 per annum gets a 3% pay rise (£24k) – it's equivalent to a doubling of pay for the average Yorkshire worker. The figure reported is almost always the ratio and never the absolute – it makes quite obscene pay rises look modest and allow the government to continue to mislead.

There is a case to be made to modify taxation, which is noted above, by substituting corporation tax with purchase tax as an example.

An argument is to give everyone a basic tax-free 'allowance' whether paid by the state or by an employer; currently to the level at which income tax begins to be paid[46].

This should simplify taxation, social support and welfare and could be developed after a couple of years of independence when the income streams and cost elements are properly established and fully understood. This is currently under discussion in Westminster, so the argument is already quite well developed.

---

[45] See Branco Milanovic *Global Inequality*.
[46] See Banerjee and Duflo.

A second approach which might be considered later is to limit company dividends payable to an individual and to set pay limits as multiples of the lowest paid worker (including zero hours).

The downside of this approach is that it will, in all probability, deter people from establishing additional businesses in the county.

Believe the experts

Today's government is littered with examples of an untutored MP over-riding the advice and knowledge of a recognised expert. Examples include:

- Climate change – despite the sea flooding whole communities, forest fires, excessive rain and unusual mildness the impact on civilisation is not being taken seriously.
- Drugs – Prof. David Nutt, a UK expert on drugs, for both medicinal and recreational use, recommended some drugs be declassified in order to reduce police time chasing and prosecuting users whilst reducing crime levels. This advice was ignored to avoid being 'politically incorrect'. Professor Nutt resigned as a government advisor – no point giving advice if some untutored biased individual can override it at a whim.
- Business Link – originally a brilliant idea that supported small businesses and innovation. A conversation between two MPs amalgamated the Business Link with all manner of organisations and launched the Small Business Service (SBS). It subsequently failed and has not been replaced by anything equally useful.

Budgeting

The current system leads to overspend in some areas with other areas neglected and the megalomaniac's belief that the bigger the budget the more important you are; so expenditure towards the financial year end rockets in order to use up the budget and ensure next year's funds plus a bit, and a bit more – if you've managed to grow your department.

The budgeting will be the reverse to what is now practiced, where departments get budgets and those budgets get broken down by region. Here we will then compile the overall budget for the county with appropriate money and resources going where most needed; not to the one who shouts loudest, or went to the right school.

Zero-based budgeting will get rid of the February road-works and accrued spending we currently enjoy and create a budget that funds both current priorities and future projects.

Allocations will be flexible, as already noted, to allow funds to be diverted from the centre to causes which need some additional attention.

Future income & expenditure

The Bank of England admitted in February 2017 that there is no way it can predict the economy beyond a few months, and neither can we; the only policy that can be reasonably adopted is to not borrow against future projections but to live off current income.

We would be no worse off than now, and there would not be the investment sucked away by Westminster to support another 'austerity' package as they continue to fill another financial gap caused by vanity projects and over-borrowing, much like the gap left by the Banksters in 2008.

Summary and Conclusions

The effect of global connectivity has all but rendered the current systems of government and economics unworkable: government focuses on alleviating poverty but ignores growing inequality. Large corporates and the rich make use of tax havens to avoid their contributions to the societies that support them.

In order for this to continue, GDP has to keep growing so that funds can be diverted to continued poverty alleviation (although the middle class get squeezed) and also to keep the notional values of stocks and shares growing so that a privileged few can ape Harry Enfield and Chums[47].

The mess that is Westminster, with hidden agendas and self-interested MPs toeing the party line in defiance of those who elected them, is likely to crumble over the next five years as we spiral into ever deeper debt with less and less trust in political decisions.

Financially, Yorkshire can be self-sufficient by using technology better, for example replacing Corporation Tax with Purchase Tax, taking the tax that is ours and applying some basic commercial principles to maintain a sound and improving society without the need to add notional value to paper[48], or for inexorable (and unsustainable?) growth in GDP.

---

[47] "I am considerably richer than you."

[48] As demonstrated by dodgy Investment Banking and the 2008 collapse where those who suffered by it are still paying and politicians yet have to legislate.

On a more local level, Yorkshire has been underfunded for decades and is expected to fund a proportion of a number of projects that will bring no benefit whatsoever to the county, but will benefit those with too much already.

A solution will be to develop a political party that supports independence for Yorkshire, managed by people with a commercial bent and supported by local elected representatives who identify the priorities by region and justify these priorities centrally on an annual basis (not 'same as last year plus a bit').

The growth in connectivity may also be used as a means of ensuring democracy by providing county-wide connectivity and downloadable apps for people to vote on local, and also county, issues as a means of directing their elected representatives.

This will not happen overnight, and there are too many examples of cobbled together political parties (gang of four, gang of seven etc.) that fall apart within a year of being formed.

The Yorkshire Democratic Party (YDP) will have clear focus and objectives in order to share a common purpose that will remain true, even in the face of changing external circumstances.

The number of representatives will be about 60, which will adequately serve the towns and rural communities but it is unlikely that more than four will be elected in 2024.

If these four can work together to be sufficiently vociferous, irritating and visible, succeeding to generate a more equal share of funding for Yorkshire the 2029 election should see a much bigger vote for the YDP and greater influence – paving the way for a truly independent county.

An option that will emerge at this point will be to offer Yorkshire as a test-bed to the failing political processes in the UK, using Westminster to provide the resources and us providing the technology to manage them.

A new Ideal:
- Continual improvement in the lifestyle of the Yorkshire people,
- A government answering to the people not as it is now with the people answering to a party,
- A focus on what matters – not notional values added to notional paper,
- Decisions based on evidence not hear-say, the whim of an individual or 'common knowledge',
- A society that can actually work to support one another,
- The four cornerstones: infrastructure, health, education & commerce managed so they work dynamically together to properly support the people and the economy,
- To generate and export tangible value,
- Adequately policed,
- Respect for the environment.

I firmly believe that, working together, to establish our own governance and independence we can significantly improve the lot of those of us lucky enough to live in this great county.

Appendices

Appendix 1
Yorkshire rules and sayings

Tha can grumble as much as tha likes – but only to thisen.
BE POSITIVE.

Tha can have bread and butter or bread and jam, tha can't have bread and butter and jam.
BE FRUGAL.

Tha can be generous to thy mates and to thisen.
BUT ONLY IN MODERATION.

There's two ways to do stuff – my way and the wrong way.
SO DO AS THA'S TOLD.

Status quo is a band, not a political ambition.
STRIVE TO DO BETTER, BE DIFFERENT AND MAKE CHANGES *(NO FAILURE, NO LEARNING)*.

You have the right to bear whippets, wear flat caps and own breweries.
YORKSHIRE IS A STATE OF MIND.

A weaver's advice to his son:

Be wary, be chary; tak 'eed who tha courts
'Cos lasses they come in all sizes and soorts
An if tha's to be 'appy, tak on wi a lass
That's nimble wi't thimble and handy wi't brass

William Beaumont. Published 1971.

A gooid way to stop a chap's maath is to keep your own shut.

A chap 'at's liberal wi' advice is generally niggardly wi' 'is brass.

John Hartley.

Our Towns:
Bradford for cash
Halifax for dash
Wakefield for pride and for poverty
Huddersfield for show
Sheffield what's low
Leeds is for dirt and vulgarity

From English Folk-Lore.
A. R. Wright. Pub 1928.

Volatile, Uncertain, Complex & Ambiguous (VUCA) – another public sector cop-out?

Preamble

Recently, in evaluating a couple of public sector post-doctoral submissions for a qualification by prior learning there was very little in the way of strategic thinking (see below) but rather a lot of reaction to external pressure. One of these very senior people considered strategy to be a response to an unfavourable article in a local newspaper.

The ensuing discussion between two postgraduate course directors, a senior moderator (with sound academic credentials), our manager and myself took the tangent that the submissions met the strategic requirements of an organisation operating in a VUCA environment. We disagreed about strategic intent.

So, I dug a bit deeper:

Fundamentals

The basic journey: Vision, Mission, Objective, Strategy, Tactics has not changed. The purpose of an organisation (its Mission) remains constant whatever the external prevailing circumstances (OK, so Nokia used to make gumboots).

The purpose of an organisation is to deliver benefit – whether to billionaire plutocrats, customers, service users or the homeless (this is elaborated in other documents).

Moving on from the delivery of benefits supports the objective (or objectives) of the organisation which, ideally, are made SMART (Specific, Measurable, Achievable, Realisable and Time-structured) and the strategy is the collection of means by which the objective(s) will be attained.

Three different strategic approaches (which can be integrated) are included as appendices.

Latterly, the notion of a two-speed environment[49] gathered some pace and probably merits more interest than it generated. In essence there is a long-term permanent core running through the organisation, its purpose and direction (a degree of certainty). Wrapped around this core is both curiosity and the need to respond to day-to-day events, some of which may be positive and should be seized or negative and should be nullified with all haste. However, it is only when the certainty has been established that curiosity or reactiveness is an acceptable activity.

<u>What is VUCA?</u>

VUCA seems to be an emerging fad that ignores the purpose of an organisation in order to focus on the fun stuff. Axiomatically, it is focused on, and can only work with, large organisations which have suitable inertia and/or not having much incentive to compete e.g. public sector, health, military – and those organisations that supply them e.g. with armaments, security or cups of tea.

---

[49] Two Speed World by Gerald Ashley & Terry Lloyd.

I tried an experiment once with a large group of erudite, people attending a function at the ICAEW (Institute of Chartered Accountants in England & Wales) when I asked 'what is the purpose of government?' – all I got were woolly answers from across the range of delegates including side-steps such as 'well, who did you vote for?', the frivolous 'to support the duck house industry' and responses around what they did e.g. 'to pass laws' – yes, but to what end? To maintain security and improve the lot of the people seemed to have been forgotten.

In effect – the public sector has somehow managed to remove any clearly defined purpose which should recognise and define the benefits delivered, and hence there is no measurable objective to inform strategy; instead we rely on policies which can be created at a whim, and usually in response to some newspaper or TV article or, at election time, as a means to curry favour.

The impact of this has been to replace strategy with policy and focus on the short-term and trivial at the expense of long-term opportunity and social development. The impact is quite clear to see where the notion of the two-speed approach has been lost in VUCA.

At February 2017 we have lost control of the prisons, we are slipping down the education ladder and shifting care for the elderly from the NHS (central government) to local communities which will, no doubt, be measured and monitored by a new army of superfluous central government inspectors who will ensure any blame is deflected well away from Whitehall.

The political short-term approach has been adapted from Rampton & Stauber's definition of political types and may be summarised as:

- The **Control Freak** who starves the organisation of real information and might use instead: - testimonials, emotionally written and with a minimum of information or, operate by developing a climate of fear through spreading uncertainty.

- The **Flooder** who maintains their position by providing too much information – often hiding contentious issues perhaps behind glittering generalities 'of course everybody knows…', or by boarding the bandwagon of a noisy action group because 'this is what *everybody* wants'.

- The **Diverter** who readily changes direction to something easier or less politically sensitive and might use a technique called 'the transfer', answering a different question to the one posed, or calling on the uninformed to contribute – because this what the 'plain folks' want.

- The **Muddier** who generates conflicting evidence to avoid a decision and might use loose words that can later be interpreted differently, or the 'soundbite' to draw attention to the trivial and away from the important or contentious.

VUCA seems to be the emerging force that transfers emphasis to the short-term horizon which is much more macho than is considered planning and it's also a lot more fun.

It also allows politicians to appear cleverer than they really are by removing the need to think, consider and make reasoned judgements that deliver benefits to a wide audience.

When I noted scenario planning to one of the VUCA advocates his response was 'what about Deepwater Horizon and the Gulf of Mexico?' - I argue that that was not scenario planning but either disaster planning or risk analysis (add Haliburton engineering and cover-up); nothing to do with scenarios, strategy or VUCA. He wasn't persuaded.

The sad bit is that this was published in the Harvard Business Review and is no doubt being picked up and peddled by noisy and flaky agencies around the world.

<u>Some concluding thoughts</u>
- VUCA is an approach that focuses on the short-term as a driver.
- VUCA has forgotten about the two-speed management of organisations.
- VUCA is an approach that risks confusing policy with strategy and replacing strategy with policy.

There doesn't appear to be any cognisance of the underlying, driving purpose of an organisation that may be used to inform strategic thinking.

Scenario planning, risk analysis and disaster recovery seem to be disciplines and approaches that are being sidelined in favour of this emerging approach.

And yes, I do think it's a cop-out for ponderous organisations to avoid or side-step their leadership obligations by shuffling obligations onto unpredictable forces.

As John Harvey Jones is reported to have said "Planning is an unnatural process: it is much more fun to do something. And the nicest thing about not planning is that failure comes as a complete surprise rather than being preceded by a period of worry and depression" – it looks like this is now being realised.

The Bank of England has recently admitted (February 2017) that there is no way they can predict the economy – despite armies of analysts and actuaries. I wonder why?

VUCA seems to have usurped the purpose of strategy to produce an approach that focuses on the whims of a few and not the benefits of the many – a bit like Kaplan & Norton repositioning Art Schneiderman's Balanced Score Card to reflect the desires of senior management, no longer to strengthen the organisation by producing a clearer understanding of market needs and expectations.

Is VUCA an emerging energetic response to the increasing importance of social media at the expense of more traditional thinking? – and being peddled by graduates who are inexperienced in business but with sound credentials in social media? – and when will the pendulum swing back again?

This is a summary of the speech given to The Academy of Social Sciences by Andrew Haldane and describes the differences in productivity.

The UK faces perhaps no greater challenge, economically and socially, than its productivity challenge. Meeting that challenge would deliver benefits to workers in improved wages and skills and to companies in greater efficiency and profitability. It would also contribute to closing inequalities of income, wealth and opportunity which have rightly and increasingly pre-occupied policymakers over recent years. The UK has a rich, in some respects world-leading, endowment of innovation and talent. This is, however, unevenly spread. Developing an institutional infrastructure, which draws on the UK's comparative advantage in innovation but which spreads its benefits more widely, would support the long tail of UK companies and the people who work for them. It would help close the pay and productivity gaps between the best and the rest, the present and the past, the in-crowd and the out. It would put the rhyme and reason back into R&D. The returns to doing so are difficult to quantify precisely. As a thought-experiment, imagine the bottom three quartiles of the UK productivity distribution saw their productivity gap with the quartile above closed. That would boost UK levels of productivity by around 13%. This would close a large part of the productivity shortfall relative to its pre-crisis trend.

And it would make inroads into closing the productivity gap with the US and Germany.

In today's prices, it would boost the level of UK GDP by around £270 billion. In closing those gaps, a useful intermediate objective would be to create in the UK a leading-edge diffusion infrastructure, to rival and complement its leading-edge innovation infrastructure. This boost our world (and, with luck, our World Cup) rankings. Inclusive innovation could serve as a conduit to inclusive growth. The UK's innovation hub would get the spokes it needs to reach every sector, every region, every worker. It would be an industrial strategy for everyone.

<u>Appendix 4 – the 'sweet-spot'</u>

Government, Society, and Industry (Corporations[50]) cannot work alone.

Business depends on society to provide purchasing power and in return rewards skills and capabilities.

Government needs industry and society for income and in return provides a license to operate and a supportive infrastructure.

Society needs government for infrastructure and industry for income.

The three key players are inextricably linked as shown in the diagram below:

---

[50] *Corporate* and *Industry* are used interchangeably

**Interdependent Responsibilities
– the parties constructively interlinked.**

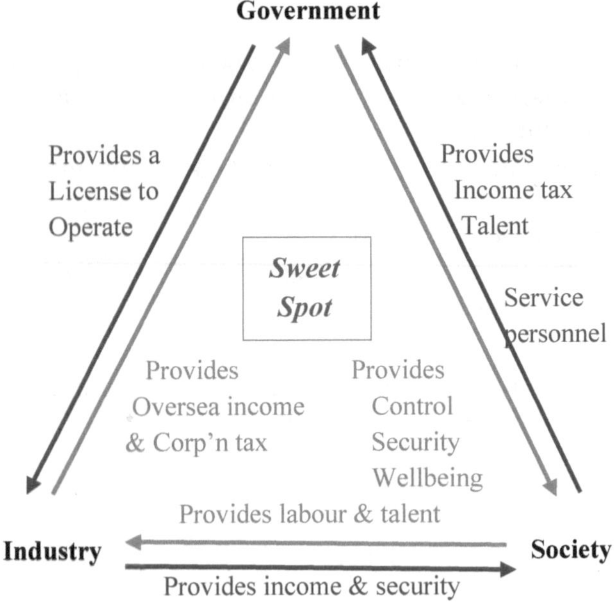

<u>Exploring the positive linkages.</u>

The Corporate ⟷ Society relationship.

Corporates and **Society:** The corporate needs to act in a responsible and supportive manner towards society for its own long-term benefit; damaging society or depleting resources can only build problems for the future.

Society and **Corporates:** Society has to help itself and despite the finer feelings of particular groups of people the world [and society] needs

130

money to operate. Society provides the skills and talent that the corporate needs in order to evolve, compete, grow and generate the wealth that makes things happen.

The Corporate ←——→ Government relationship.

Corporates and **Government:** it is the corporate that is the fundamental source of sustainable income to government through taxes on sales, corporation tax and indirectly through the income tax the workforce pays.

Government and **Corporates:** government gives corporates a license to operate and the framework in which to operate responsible business; too much regulation causes creativity and competitiveness to falter, too little regulation and there's always Jack the Lad to take advantage of the weak or unwary.

Government ←——→ Society relationship.

Government and **Society:** rarely do we think about the purpose of government [answer on page 10] yet government manages and regulates society; if this is done irresponsibly or in an unequal manner [reduced social mobility, loss of access, bankers' bonuses for example] society is undermined and weakened as a result and sustainability has been eroded.

Society and **government:** Society provides income tax to help pay for governance and also furnishes the talent to run government well, deliver public services and protect our shores.

And, all this can be brought together in a *Sweet Spot* where each of the players support one another.

Some of the negative impacts of interdependency.

When Society breaks down.

One extreme example of societal breakdown is the rioting seen around 2012 where businesses got trashed and there are huge costs in policing and infrastructure replacement – commerce and government suffer as a result.

The UK Guardian newspaper in August 2011 analysed the reasons behind the riots and identified a number of close correlations, two have been selected to illustrate the point:

- ".... appears to confirm that the accused are overwhelmingly young, male and unemployed" – Business failing to deliver work.
- "... while education attainment was significantly lower." – Government failing to deliver education.

When Government breaks down.

When governments break down, commerce and society suffer as a result.

The *Fund for Peace* describes a failed state [government] quite comprehensively, and which Wikipedia summarises as:

"...the common characteristics of a failing state include a central government so weak or ineffective

that it has little practical control over much of its territory.

> - *non-provision of public services;* [failing to support society].
> - *refugees and involuntary movement of populations;* [damaging society].
> - *widespread corruption and criminality;* [taking from society and business].
> - *and sharp economic decline"* [not supporting business].

When Commerce breaks down.

The impact of commerce breaking down is business closures – where society and government suffer as a result.

- Business closures inevitably lead to subsequent lay-offs, which damages society.

- Falling revenues and growing margins lead to loss of tax revenue [and often increased off-shoring] which damages government.

<u>We cannot operate in isolation.</u>

For too long governments have sat back and acted as 'policemen', judging the probity of its citizens and standing aloof. At the time of writing [August 2012] a recent programme created by *Sky News 'Born Bankrupt'* is a damning indictment of a government sitting back, observing and failing to act [interestingly there are very few interviews with politicians – who are normally the first to mount the soapbox]. Government has acted in isolation and failed to support its citizens and its industry in the longer term.

Business, likewise, more and more concentrates on short-term returns and has failed to invest in itself, its people or the society in which it operates. Some years ago, there was a study that compared major stock-market quoted companies with major companies that were either unquoted or mostly owned by the founders [a good example today is Mars]. The differences were significant over the longer term, with the 'private' companies significantly outperforming those whose shares were freely traded.

There are examples too of societies that have operated in isolation, China being a good example; closing out the world for many centuries and eventually being subject to extreme poverty. Upon embracing the world, their economy has grown substantially and poverty reduced although not eliminated. The opening up was to industry and with recognition of other governments [Hong Kong once acting as a gateway – see below].

Some of the positive impacts of interdependency.

On a more positive note, there are examples of significant success where all three parties work together from a position of trust and have due regard for each others' capabilities where they may not have appropriate experience [how many politicians have actually worked in industry, how many people have participated in government and how many industrialists have their main residence in high density towns and cities].

There are examples of 'sovereign cities' where the rules [governance] are different from the country of which they are a part.

In such cities free trade is encouraged, finances are sound, taxation is controlled and guaranteed and ambitious, challenging and creative people are welcomed.

The original model was Lübeck on the north coast of Germany which was described as one of the 'five glories of the empire' by Charles IV [discussed in more detail in the excellent book *Adapt* by *Tim Harford*]. Venice and Florence operated in similar fashion and modern day examples include Hong Kong, Singapore and Shenzhen; Dubai is a similar area with non-oil trade growing 12% p.a. [See Gulfnews.com]. Each of these areas has different rules to the 'parent' country and independently managed economies.

By working together and recognising the others' needs, Corporate, Social and Governmental responsibility creates a very positive and rich environment for all those involved.

A simple conclusion.

Properly applied Corporate [Societal and Governmental] Responsibility, which addresses and incorporates the needs of others can demonstrably continue to make a profit, strengthen society and support government.

But, as Tim Harford comments when discussing the economist Paul Romer who wants to develop the *Charter City* concept [a modern day Lübeck] using Guantanamo Bay as a fanciful example:

"...Cuba, the USA and Canada agree to transfer Guantanamo Bay to the Canadians, who establish a Hong Kong in the Caribbean: the Cubans gain a gateway to twenty-first century capitalism; the Americans rid themselves of a public-relations problem; the Canadians gain influence and wealth. Economically this is plausible. Politically it is almost inconceivable".

<u>Appendix 5; the Original 2009 Paper</u>

The purpose of government?
– a bit of a moan but with a few thoughts.

<u>Introduction</u>
Some time ago I wondered *'what is the* real *purpose of government?'* and started to ask people who should know; I was met with answers that began to define functionality – but not purpose:

- To make laws,
- To ensure people comply,
- To manage infrastructure,
- To raise revenue.

Eventually after much digging, I got to:

"To ensure the safety of the realm, to improve the circumstances of those within the realm and to maintain a system of effective democracy now and into the future".

<u>An answer that actually defines purpose.</u>
So, let's explore some of what has happened:

- Due to <u>too much</u> political intervention outside their areas of responsibility – overseas – We are less secure than we have been since the second world war.

We are less secure due to the threat of terrorism, and also in terms of energy since we wasted the North Sea opportunity and became beholden to overseas suppliers.

- Due to <u>a lack of</u> political intervention we have seen our savings tumble, house prices collapse[51] and sound businesses fold whilst those responsible continue to live well either through their earlier mismanagement, or secure in their public sector jobs.

When debt repayment is taken into account and lack of liquidity in the country as a whole, we are surely less well-off than we have been since the Second World War.

- Due to <u>avoiding the issues</u>, lies and incompetence have been hidden under spin and deceit that has been taken to a new level as a means to avoid issues or postpone making meaningful decisions.

Never has there been less accountability with fewer decisions, other than to go with the populist press in order to be 'everyone's friend'.

It is this spineless management that led to the significant industrial unrest when we once had a manufacturing presence.

<u>And what is being done now that we:</u>

- Have squandered our ability to make things, other than books and films,
- Have lost the will to trade goods and services,
- Are tied up in pointless bureaucracy,
- Have some 900,000 supernumerary pen pushers and regulators, hired to keep down unemployment figures – and who will attract pensions in the future.

---

[51] This was written in 2009, just after the collapse.

It was said some 30 years ago that the UK was being reduced to selling insurance and hamburgers to each other with no sustainable source of revenue inflow.

We've sold whatever productive capacity we had to overseas companies which can readily repatriate profits.

We support off-shoring; which is money laundering by any other name, legitimised so that those with money (including the corporations) can keep their money.

At a recent lecture it was reported that the top 50% of UK GDP (from the FT 500) contribute just 8% of corporation tax; the other 50% of GDP (the SMEs) contribute the other 92%!

But it's worse than that – we are being exhorted to buy Chinese, Japanese, Korean and Indian goods to exacerbate the flow of funds from the country (is this to generate VAT and other taxes to support government, yet impoverish the country as a whole?)

And, Dubai is looking increasingly popular as a place to site the stock exchange, which is the one significant source of revenue that we still have, and that's pretty suspect as things stand at the moment.

We have diluted our culture and heritage with Christmas trees now becoming 'holiday trees' stopped kids playing conkers, banned egg & spoon and pancake races in case someone gets hurt, and we have a voting system that favours actors and sycophants in place of people who know what they're actually doing.

Some Conclusions

Our politicians have failed us on every front – yes, they're good with words, blame and cover-up but the inescapable conclusion is that in 'performing' their public duties they have succeeded in making this nation:

- More open now to terrorism,
- Worse off now than for over 40 years,
- Less secure in the future for energy supplies,
- Impoverished in the future as borrowings and unnecessary index-linked pensions will need to be paid,
- Possibly abandoned in the future as our one source of significant revenue goes to Dubai for reasons of personal taxation,
- Suffering under climate change because of pandering to paid lobbyists and the wealthy,
- One that is managed by actors and lawyers in place of people with genuine business skill or entrepreneurial competence.

Some thoughts about possible solutions

Measure What Matters, Not Anything That Moves.

Decide what is actually important for the nation – not for those in government. As an example, the cost of admin should be between 16% and 25% of turnover/income; for a global company it's about

17%, for the old Business Link about 55% (a criminal waste of public money, simply because no-one had provided a clear mandate).

<u>Provide Genuine Support for Small Business.</u>
How about putting back the Business Links under commercial management, not run by career politicians, or their old school pals?

<u>Decision-Making.</u>
Explore the substance of government promises – easily made, rarely delivered – why?

A decision involves commitment, and if held off for long enough, any decision becomes a good one[52]. To a competent manager the purpose of a decision is to make the problem smaller; to a politician, focused on appearance rather than reality, the purpose of a decision is to push the eventuality into the distance, so that it just looks smaller.

The major outputs are announcements that sound good but never lead anywhere. Some incisive decision-making would be a welcome change from dither and spin.

<u>Teamwork.</u>
Will Schutz, who developed FIRO-B (to simplify) identified three stages that successful teams will go through: common purpose, authority with responsibility then openness.

---

[52] See the *International Journal of Management and Decision Making* Vol. 6, Nos. 3/4 pg 372 ff.

Our politicians are so interested in what's in it for themselves (explore the issues over expenses and their being declared); how many MPs (and MEPs) have been reprimanded for unethical use of public funds, yet none have been fired or told to pay back the money – they simply get barred from the House for a couple of weeks (paid holiday).

A start point might be to demand total transparency, where those people acting with devastating incompetence or illegally (as in commerce) are fired and their ill-gotten gains confiscated.

One example might be second mortgages on London homes paid from the public purse; on retirement, or cessation of office, those properties revert to the treasury – not the individual's bank account.

<u>Stop Tinkering.</u>
Eurofighter – late, the dome – over budget, Wembley – an embarrassment.

Unofficially, a major UK civil engineer turned down the opportunity to build the new Wembley Stadium because they knew that such a high profile project would attract all and sundry determined to leave 'a legacy' and result in over-runs, delays and re-builds in order to accommodate people with little or no understanding of the project.

On the other hand, a significant rebuild on a Crown property (£70m+) was managed to time by challenging the politicians and meddlers with 'good ideas' that their ideas would delay the project and no doubt upset the Queen and their knighthoods.

Pity the Queen isn't involved in more high profile projects involving tax-payers' money.

Make Off-shoring Illegal.
With the top 50% of GDP delivering 8% of taxation, off-shoring could be made illegal and as a conservative estimate, this could boost the exchequer by about 25%.

Some people might argue that good companies would go abroad, but then if a company isn't paying the right tax, or is foreign owned (repatriating profits) is this an argument of any substance?

A similar argument exists with wealthy individuals: we could lose them if tax regimes are unfavourable, but many of them are already officially UK residents for less than 150 days a year and so avoid tax as non-domiciled.

Make Taxation Simple.
Separate taxation from National Insurance (NI). Tax may be used to run the government machine; NI may be used to pay for hospitals, pensions and the things that go to caring for people. It would also make absolutely clear the wastage that goes on in government – see below and the cost of social support.

Reduce the Civil Service.
Alan Clark (the MP who lived in a castle) pointed out over 20 years ago that you could lose an entire layer of Whitehall and no-one would notice; this was riposted by another MP to the effect that

"government is an inherently wasteful process" – this then makes everything OK.

Given inherent wastefulness, the public sector can continue with no pressure to be efficient, unlike the private sector that pays their wages and pensions. This is a mind set that should be addressed, and could be started by adopting zero based budgeting.

Jobseekers allowance will no doubt be cheaper in the long run than their on-going salaries and the pensions accumulating from the years yet to be worked.

Actually Take On The EU. [*2009 remember*]

Too often we have rolled over and accepted the rulings of Brussels however damaging and costly; these people should be held to account and, if they fall short, we withhold their payments – it's surely crazy to pay for services we don't receive and support people who don't deliver.

Provide Support for Society.

Make money directly available for borrowings, and cash flow.

It could open the way to give a lease of life to the Post Offices whilst ensuring government policy is properly administered. At the same time putting a bit of pressure on the High street banks to act responsibly for once.

Some Initiatives?

<u>Turn the Bank of England into a lending bank.</u>
The government now owns, or more or less owns: RBS, Northern Rock and the Post Office; sufficient outlets and coverage, staffed by experts to provide basic bank lending and savings, mortgages, unemployment benefit and pensions.

If depositors could be indemnified (would this be cheaper than the enormous bail-outs that still haven't run their course) and the government runs a saving and lending arm the High Street banks can either sort themselves out (big bonuses and all) – or go to the wall.

Ignore Brussels claiming it's anti-competitive – just as the Italians would do, let the lawyers spend the next five years earning fat fees whilst nothing happens and we get out of this problem and let the other recalcitrant banks sort themselves out.

There might even be a decent bonus for the taxpayer as 'The Bank' attracts increasing numbers of customers and rising share value to deliver good dividends and a significant return when put back into private ownership.

<u>Hospitals</u>
Let's forget about equal opportunities, and the inability to discipline without fear of reprisal and bring back a matron who has some real authority.

<u>Education</u>
Let's unashamedly bring back: streaming, English grammar and discipline – not just for the pupils but

also the teachers, perhaps dressing as if they mean business not as someone returning from their morning jog.

Industry

Support invention at the SME level, much of the support is tied to education (often slow and unaware of commercial confidence) or to big companies that can handle the significant administration needed to justify a government grant[53].

Much innovation is in the SME sector, but not accessible due to lack of development – Dyson is typical, going to Japan for support then Hoover tried to copy (losing the subsequent court case) and Trevor Baylis is quite vitriolic about government's lack of understanding and support for innovation.

The Prison Service

Equal opportunities, personal dignity and all those regulations that take away direct management intervention should be removed on entering the prison, a big number of released prisoners re-offend, there should be some swing of the pendulum back from rehabilitation to some punishment.

Secondly, on reoffending, double the sentence that would have been applied and keep doing so. For example the persistently offending motorist is

---

[53] One SME declined the £40,000 needed to develop a new carbon fibre application as it did not have the resources to properly administer to the required level of detail

banned for three months, then six months, and then is caught shoplifting which would normally carry one month in jail now becomes four months.

After a period of overcrowding, the message should get through and the prison population begin to see sense and decline in numbers. After a couple of times being caught, people might think a third time about re-offending.

<u>Favours and Promises</u>

Some of politics operates through 'favour banks' – helping other politicians during the (technically necessary?) overseas trips. Is it possible that some of these favours and promises create imaginary barriers to new initiatives and could be suspended?

Where to start?

There are a good many more possible initiatives than those mentioned above, for example ***defence of the realm*** is only touched upon in the <u>stop tinkering</u> thoughts, and democracy isn't mentioned other than obliquely in <u>favours and promises</u>.

Whilst there are some thoughts about society, society will not function without the support of government and industry, so surely the key is to get overseas trade moving to generate foreign currency, provide work and improve the lot of the population. We're good at invention (carbon fibre noted at footnote 4) and the creative arts (Harry Potter); we're no longer good at mass manufacture, other than very specialist items such as Burberry or Rolls Royce.

So, in order of priority wouldn't it make sense to:

- Turn the Bank of England into a lending bank using RBS, Northern Rock and the Post Office,
- Remove the overburdening bureaucracy needed to manage even quite modest innovation grants[54] and reduce the Civil Service element needed to administer these grants (Parkinson's Law again),
- Make funds readily available for development, then funds for prototyping, then for production.

The thorny problems of ego, waste and accumulating pensions can be tackled some time later.

Steve Mullins
January 2009

Addendum

Latterly, the issue of the Post Office being part privatised is surely another example of lack of control.

---

[54] And accept that there will be some misappropriation of funds, but not to the cost of the government audit process or the time taken to complete the paperwork.

The Post Office is a public body run by the government who should control, oversee or provide competent trustees for the workers' pensions.

Surely Lord Mandleson's threats about loss of pension rights if not part privatised is a screaming admission of yet more financial incompetence, and a bail-out would be a drop in the ocean compared to the burden being built for future generations.

A select Bibliography

A collection of some of the books which have helped develop the ideas in this book. The authors are in no way responsible for how I have interpreted their words.

Arranged alphabetically by Surname.

Gerald Ashley & Terry Lloyd. *Two Speed World*. ISBN 978-1906659707.

Abhijit Bannerjee and Esther Duflo. *Good Economics for Hard Times; (better answers to our biggest problems)*. ISBN 978-0-241-30689-5.

Richard Barker. *Determining Value*. ISBN 0-273-63979-X.

Frederick Brookes, *The Mythical Man Month*. ISBN 978-0-20183-595-3.

Peter Dauvergne. *Will Big Business Destroy our Planet?* ISBN 978-0-5095-2401-3.

DEFRA. *Landscapes Review*, Sept 2019. see in particular *Proposal 18*.

Mitch Feierstein. *Planet Ponzi*. ISBN 978-0-552-77827-5.

Ian Griffiths. *New Creative Accounting.* ISBN 0-333-62865-9.

Tim Harford. *Adapt.* ISBN 978-0-349-12151-2.

Institute for Business Ethics. *Does Business Ethics Pay?* ISBN 0-9539517-3-1.

Digby Jones & Michael Wilson. *Fixing Britain.* ISBN 978-0-470-97763-7.

Owen Jones. *The Establishment.* ISBN 978-0-141-97499-6.

Steve Keen. *Debunking Economics.* ISBN 978-1-84813-992-3.
Steve Keen. *Can we Avoid Another Financial Crisis?* ISBN 978-1-5095-1373-4.

Quentin Letts. *Patronising Bastards.* ISBN 978-1-4721-2735-8.

Branco Milanovic. *Global Inequality.* ISBN 978-0-674-98403-5.

Steve Mullins. *Beyond Money.* ISBN 978-1-78955-828-9.
Steve Mullins. *International Journal of Management and Decision-Making. Vol 6. 2005.* Pages 372 – 381. ISSN 1462-4621 (Print). 1741-5187 (on-line).

C. Northcote Parkinson. *Parkinson's Law*. ISBN 0-14-009107-6.

Robert Peston. *WTF*. ISBN 978-1-473-66130-1.

Sheldon Rampton & John Stauber. *Trust us, We're Experts*. ISBN 1-58524-139-1.

Steve Richards. *The Rise of the Outsiders*. ISBN 978-1-78649-1428.

James Rickards. *The New Case for Gold*. ISBN 978-0-241-24835-5.
James Rickards. *The Road to Ruin*. ISBN 978-0-241-18920-7.

Josh Ryan-Collins, Tony Greenham, Richard Werner, Andrew Jackson. *Where Does Money Come From?* ISBN 978-1-521-04389-9.

Will Schutz. *The Human Element*. ISBN 1-55542-612-3.

Tim Steer. *The Signs Were There*. ISBN 978-1-78816-0803.

Professional Manager, Spring 2019. *E-Stonia, how these two men built a digital nation*. Pp.43-47.

Meet the author

I am no politician; I'm a manager with a background firmly rooted in commerce and industry.

Here's a potted history.

* Born & raised in Birkenshaw, West Riding.
* Liverpool University, degrees in biology and
    ecology.

<u>Commercial Beginnings</u>
* Express Foods.
  * Research & Development. New products, factory
      installation and commissioning of new plant.
  * Marketing. Catering market, increased turnover
      significantly.
* Mars, Catering & Vending.
  * Development. New services, new products.
  * Market Development. Primarily UK, France &
      Germany.
* Gallaher, Marketing & Development.
  * Take opportunities from concept to market, make
      profitable and integrate into core business.
  * Business defence, protected 650 jobs and £70m
      turnover.

<u>Morton Hodson. Business Consultancy</u>, SME focus.
* Enterprise Initiatives: strategy, marketing & export

<u>Focus Consulting, Partnership</u>.
* Commended for transport company strategy
    (sustainable 20% profit improvement).

- Upper quartile for business advisors in the south east.
- Delivered ethics training to Police Strategic Command (Bramshill).

<u>Self-employed</u>.
- Instrumental in evolving the West London Business Link from the local TEC,
- Winner of Barclays *Building Better Business Award,*
- Regional Finalist of Shell's *Making the Difference Award,*
- Business Link, Personal Business Advisor.
  - Tripled the profit for a specialist printer,
  - Food company grew 25% per annum compound, from 64 staff,
  - Helped architect grow from 2 people to 15 with office move.

<u>Ascot Associates</u> (my own company).
- Diagnostic saved £500,000 for a high-profile service company,
- Met. Police analysis working with Young People At Risk,
- Marked and moderated management qualifications for the CMI.

<u>Some Past Memberships:</u>
- Institute for Business Ethics,
- Fellow of the Royal Society of Arts,
- Chartered Marketer,
- Certificated Management Consultant (Fellow).

Publications:

How to Market Yourself in a Week. ISBN 978-0-957340-3-9. Gaining a new job (from outplacement experience) – the practices also apply to business growth.

The Story of Cash Flow. ISBN 978-0-9576340-2-2. As far as I can tell, the world's first commercial fairy story and a guide to the pitfalls for someone setting up in business.

Beyond Money. ISBN 978-1-78955-828-9. A guide to Sustainable Business. Collected papers written over many years that explore and expand an holistic business model.

In conjunction with Vince Golder: The Consummate Professional's Guide to Referral Marketing. ISBN 978-1-78955-339-0. Ideas and processes to get others to do your selling for you.

www.ingramcontent.com/pod-product-compliance
Lightning Source LLC
Chambersburg PA
CBHW031119250726
48655CB00004B/1768